Disclaimer

Everything you read in this book are stories of true life events. These events are life events of the author. I have changed the names of people in this story and not given out any real information to identify anybody. I do not wish to disclose the names of my abusers, as this would reopen closed doors and give them attention.

Rest assured that these people will be punished by karma, and there is no longer any public action needed; Nor could it help.
The events did happen in rural Kentucky. The time frame for the events and locations are also true. I wished to publish my childhood story and share it with the world in hopes that people out there who have lived through what I have, or worse, know that they are not alone. I will not come forth publicly and I do not want media publicity. Do not harass me for more information. You will receive no further information from me.

Pain- A memoir

By Mick S Bear

To the light of my life, my darling wife.

1. "Baby on ice"

I guess the title of this chapter pretty much sums up most of my life. While I laugh at it now, being thrown in a baby carseat in the dead of winter across an icy porch by your psychotic mother doesn't seem like such a traumatic incident. Looking at it from a moral perspective however leaves a lot to be desired.

What type of person does that to a 3 month old infant?

She was upset that I was crying, and so she packed my belongings at the ripe age of 3 months old. Headed out to my grandmother's sometime around the dead of winter, and proceeded to "hand" me over to my grandmother.

By hand, I mean the woman was outright pissed off at the fact that she would rather spend her time partying with her friends than being tied down with the product of a broken marriage. Her and my father weren't seeing eye to eye and would soon divorce.

So mom, being the wise eighteen year old that she was, took me to my grandmother.

With a hard thrust and a "You keep the little crying motherf*cker." She proceeded to teach me how to ice skate from a carseat.

Needless to say, I don't remember a thing. To be completely honest, I really don't remember anything of the incident. Now, mind you, my grandmother had came and found me months earlier from the old trailer my mom was renting somewhere in the small town she grew up.

Grandma found me in a soiled diaper, in an empty trailer with my mother nowhere in sight.

She packed what belongings I had and took me out of that godforsaken trailer.

I guess mom didn't have a problem with it because she didn't come to claim me until a few weeks later, but didn't keep me long.

She sent me on ice not long after that. I must've been a natural at it because I only did it once.

Mom disappeared. I hadn't seen her in over 3 years after that. Birthdays came and went, and I didn't see mom. Unknown to me at the time in all my wisdom at two years old, mom was in jail.

Pregnant with my other brother, Lakota; who I'll talk about later.

Mom had been hanging out with my brother's father late one night, after having been living out of a vehicle and bathing in the local creek while subsisting off of cigarettes and bologna sandwiches.

Anyways, Mom and him were scoping a house out in the middle of the night. He assured mom that he was living with a guy in the house and that he had forgotten some possessions in the house. Her,

being naive and young, trusted what he said.
He must've not known the house he was
burglarizing wasn't empty because when the sheriff
showed up moments later both my mother and him
were charged with a felony.
She was hauled off to jail that night where she
spent many months, all the while pregnant with
"Bub". (Which is what he'll be called from now on).
When mom returned as I was turning three, she
surprised me. I am sure I was glad at the time to
see mom. Seems like I was more confused where
she was to be honest.
My grandma spoke of me watching "The Land
Before Time" and touching the television and crying
for my mother at two years old. It was because I
thought my mother died just like Littlefoot's and I
didn't know where she was.
When mom returned, she stayed with my grandma
a little while, along with my newly born baby
brother.
Legend has it that from the moment we met, I didn't
like him. I guess that carried on for years after, well
into adulthood.
Don't get me wrong, I love him now, but we don't
see eye to eye on a lot of things.
He was always the outlaw and I the future "police
officer" which by the way, ended up never
happening.

Mom left my grandma's house not long after a few
months. She had been working at a truck stop up in
the city, and had met someone. They both shacked

up in a trailer park in the city, and took my brother with them.

I stayed with grandma as I had become so attached to her that they had trouble getting me to stop crying. Must've been abandonment issues or something.

Around this time, life became a blur to me. I have faint memories of visiting mom's trailer. At one point she took me from my grandmother for a few months. I obviously didn't adapt well to this and found myself sad quite often.

One memory that stands out to me is around 4 years old, my grandma pulled up in the trailer park and I ran up to her car. I remember being so happy to see her, I wanted to go home with her.

What ended up happening though, is that while mom agreed that I could go stay with her, I had to be back the next day.

Grandma visited well into the night, and then she took me to the store with her and "Papaw" who was my non-biological grandfather, but in my eyes always has been.

We walked around the aisles and she allowed me to get a lunchable. As a little kid, lunchables were like getting diamonds or gold. Kids love that shit, and I was no exception.

My grandparents spent way too long in the store and I ended up falling asleep on the way home to my grandmothers. It was a very long drive and took well over an hour from the part of the city my mother lived in as grandma lived in a little shack out in rural Kentucky.

I remember waking up the next morning at my grandma's while my grandpa placed the lunchable in my hand he fetched from the fridge. I remember the sad feeling of wanting my grandma, but she had left for work that day.

Grandpa took me back to the city, and I'm sure I cried all the way. It would be unlike me if I didn't, because I was always attached to my grandparents like they were actually my own parents. It stems from being basically raised by them.

I'll never forget when grandpa's truck pulled up and he took me up to the door and I went in.

Mom was asleep, I remember that. I remember feeling so alone and afraid.

Grandpa drove off and left me to my demise, all with the lunchable still in my hand.

To me, this lunchable was a gift from my precious grandmother and it meant very much to me.

However, as I was unable to open it, I sat it down on the coffee table.

Sometime after that, between bouts of obnoxious crying, I fell asleep. I awoke hours later to some strange lady and my mom talking, the woman had ate my lunchable.

Now, this woman was a friend of my mother and went by the name Rose. She was a very strange woman to me. She talked slow, and smelled really bad of cigarettes.

She sometimes had foam at the corners of her mouth. Mom assured me that ants had gotten into my lunchable and so she gave it to Rose.
This was obviously a flat out lie to cover up the fact that it crushed my spirit to lose such a precious gift from my grandparents. Maybe she told me this to ease the burden of knowing she betrayed her son for a mere 'friend'.

Fast forward a few months and my mother returned me to my grandma. I remained in her custody for the next two years until right before kindergarten.
Mom at this point relocated to a house back in our hometown, closer to my grandmother.
She told me I was going to come live with her, and I told her I didn't want to.
Knowing mom now, I'm sure she said something along the lines of "too bad." As would be typical of her.
Kindergarten took off without a hitch, I made friends and enemies. Of all the details my memory isn't that great. I do remember my mother waiting for me at grandma's one afternoon.
I hopped off the bus and she greeted me with a "Pack your stuff, you're coming to live with me."
I can only imagine the horrified look on my face.
Grandma would've stopped her but she wasn't home at the time as she worked. And before you

think I normally got off the bus alone, understand that my aunt lived with my grandmother, and still does to this day.
Aunt D.D. as she was referred to by us children. Anyway, she would've been no help against my mother's wishes as she wasn't exactly thrilled about having to raise her sister's kids.

Mom took me away that day, against my will. Little did I know my whole world would be turned upside down. This was going to be the years of my life that I remembered the most. The first time in my life I would ever be violently beaten, starved and verbally abused. At five-and-a-half, I was everything but aware of the hellish life I'd have for the next 3 years.
When mom rolled up to the old red house off of 31W, in the small fenced in lot among other houses, God only knows what the hell I was thinking.

If I had to guess what I was thinking, it was probably about grandma's.

2. "Welcome to my world, bitch."

Upon entering the house I was defiant against my captor. I didn't want to be there and I told her that. Mom wasn't having that. She picked me up and began striking me with her hand on my backside. She then threw me to the floor and afterwards made me stand in the corner.

"I hate you!" I cried. "Good." She resounded. Basically telling me that I was going to stay with her and "Fuck your granny."

The rest of that day was a blur, and the days to follow.

I ended up not seeing my grandma for quite a while. Someone who I loved like my very own mother, just up and gone from my life. I was hurt, I was afraid.

I was so little, my brain didn't comprehend my mother. I knew she was mom, because I had been told that. Realistically, my mother was my grandma. Mom knew that "granny" had been my rock and shelter. She was jealous of that. She hated it.

I have "fond" memories of my mother rocking back and forth on the couch while sipping whiskey and coke all the while listening to the radio. Something I was told she did nearly all her life, minus the alcohol.

One particular day, I was trying to make Kool-aid for my mother. As she sat in the living room rocking, I was in the kitchen trying to pour a glass of Kool-aid for her. It being too heavy for my scrawny six-year-old frame, I accidentally dropped the pitcher, covering the entire kitchen floor with Kool-aid.

Mom came up off that couch, smacked me in the face so hard that I recoiled to the floor and she proceed to stand over me and hit me as I rolled into the fetal position to protect my head. She spoke through her teeth at me about being "retarded", "stupid" and something else.

I laid in a pool of red Kool-aid, crying. As any kid would be in this situation, I was very shaken. I just wanted to make mama something to drink.

This was the first of many instances of abuse that I endured. I have memories of my mother approaching me while biting her lip and talking through her teeth like a demon. Scared the hell out of me as a child. She encouraged my step dad to beat the hell out of me too, and he did so often. One time she sliced my face with her fingernail over me not cleaning my room properly.

As this was a nightmare to me, at this point, things began to feel natural. I didn't tell anybody because I thought all kids had this stuff done to them. It just wasn't something I thought would've been taboo. One day I pissed mom off for tying my shoes wrong. She slammed me to the floor and stomped my back and told me she was going to kill me when I got home from school. I believed her so much that I went to school and sat quietly in class. My first grade teacher approached me on the recess yard and asked me what was wrong. "Mama said she

was going to kill me." After I said this, tears began
to flow down my cheeks.

Mrs. Phillips took me straight away to the principal
office where they contacted child protective
services and reassured me that everything was
going to be okay. Boy, they were sure fucking
wrong.

Later that day, as I went to get off the bus, I knew
mom found out I told. The bus driver wouldn't let
me off the bus until social services arrived.

The social worker came to the bus stop and took
me off the bus. She then walked me up to that red
dungeon we called 'home' and my mother was
already outside.

Mom of course, was extra polite. She was also
super nice to me, and my dumbass believed she
was being genuine.

"All I ever do is discipline my kids with a paddle."
My mother said. "It's my christian beliefs." Was
another cop out she used. The social worker said
that was understandable (something that doesn't fly
by today's standards) and questioned my mom
about the death threat.

Mom denied it, but I mean, who the hell wouldn't
deny that? She was running risk of losing her kid,
and potentially facing abuse charges.

Looking back, that was well what my mother
deserved.

The social worker believed everything checked out,
and mom was really putting on a show. Using
humor and playing everything off, while holding me

close like she loved me dearly. Social services bought it all, everything mom was selling. All the bullshit.

Hell, I bought it too. Up until the social worker left.

I was told to go out and play by my mother at some point. So, thinking nothing of it, I ran outside to play while her and the social worker remained in the house to talk.

I still remember to this day riding on my littlest brother's trike in the front yard when my friend from school who lived next door yelled across the fence for me to come play.

"I'll be right there in a minute, Dakota!" I yelled as loud as I could.

The social worker left shortly after, and my mother came outside.

I remember asking her if I could go to Dakota's to play. "Get in the house." she said to me. The look in her eyes, I had seen before. Too many times. I knew I was in trouble. I didn't know what I had done was wrong. "You're a fucking little lying bastard!" She yelled as I went into the living room with her following close behind. A slap to the face, and another and another.

I got sent to bed without food or water that night and threatened if I ever did it again, she would let the state take me and I would never see my granny again. This was a heavy wager to me, and so from that moment forth, I defended my abusers and excused their abuse.

Mom took me out of school not long after that. I never finished 1st grade. Most of my life at that point consisted of being locked out every morning in my white briefs and barefoot while I ran around outside with my little brother Lakota all day. He and I played together like that all the time, except mom let him go inside when he was hungry and thirsty.
I remember encouraging him to steal food for me in the kitchen, and he did. Bub always knew mom favored him and he played it to his advantage quite often.
Most times getting his way with her either by throwing a fit or just being himself; he always was a card. Always trying to be funny; he was just a goof ball.
One incident I was swinging in a swing in the backyard when my mom opened the back door. She made my brother and I a small pizza each.

I dropped mine to which she told me to "Fucking starve, bitch."
She locked the back door again, and that was that. So here I was, at six going on seven, being hated by someone who spawned me into this world.
Then, having the audacity to blame me for my own existence. That's mom for you.

3. "Stepdad from hell"

As a kid, if you combined Hitler with Stalin, this man was a mean little sonofawhore. This man was a straight up piece of dog scut you'd find on the bottom of your shoe. Standing five-foot-six and one-hundred-fifty pounds, he was a mean drunk who made our lives a living hell. Us kids, and our mother.
How my mom found the piece of shit (Oh yeah, at a truck stop) is beyond me. What she saw in this little loudmouth was invisible because I was still looking, and so was my grandma.
He dished out alot our beatings, both with ping pong paddles on our rear ends to wooden fish scaling boards (one of which was broken on my back) to bare open hands upside the head.
He was heartless towards me and my brother. Absolutely hated us because we were the children of our mother's prior flings. A reminder of her sexually driven past.
Being the insecure and inferior little prick that he was, he once had the nerve to threaten me with an extension cord. I feared this man greatly, as I'd been beaten with flurries of open handed slaps all over my body.
He hit me like he would a man. Bub and I both were subject as his punching bags.
Never will forget the time I got sick all over my bed sheets and he made me go out in the snow late one night all while wearing my tighty whities and scraping my sheets off barehanded.

This actually happened. A six year old boy barefoot in the snow at eight o'clock at night trying to scrape puke off of a sheet while barely being able to keep my head up.
Mom thought this too far, go figure. She allowed me to come back inside.
There was times when mom and he would get into fights, and he would choke her and punch her in the face with his fist. This man was a monster in my childlike eyes. He was able to beat my mother, and to me she was a demon. How much more so did I fear him because he was able to beat her. This made him much more scary to me.

One night, Bub and I were in our back bedroom. We heard a commotion coming from the front of the house. We looked to find our stepfather with his shotgun out. There on the kitchen table sat a bottle of beer and a bottle of tylenol.
Mom and him had been fighting, and she decided she had been through enough of his abuse.
He threatened to kill himself if she tried to leave.
She told him to "Go ahead and do it." which definitely was okay in my book at the time too. As sad as it seems for a child, watching him toss the shotgun to the side and him dump a handful of tylenol in his hand and then swallow large amounts was satisfying.
He then turned up the beer and chugged it while my mom began to panic. She was begging him to stop and by this point, it was too late.
She ran for the phone and told us kids that he was

going to die. I thought this funny as a kid. I wanted him to. All the mean shit he did, to my brother and I, he deserved to.

Paramedics arrived after sometime, and he was laying in the living room. He was convulsing and I remember the paramedics administer some type of black fluid.
He spent nearly two weeks on the couch unable to move or talk. He didn't eat and barely drank water. He came so close to death that it was too good to be true.

Just as I began to feel sorry for him, he got better. My brother soon told him that I had been excited about him dying. This infuriated our step dad so much that he proceeded to hit me in the face with his slaps.

This only further made him hate me. One day after having failed to rinse the dishes properly, he decided he was going teach me a lesson.
He called for me into the kitchen, and when I showed up he told me to put my hands on the back of the chair.
This was a common practice in our house, right before you received a spanking. You gripped the back of the chair so you wouldn't be able to reflex in time to stop the board from striking your rear end.
Mainly so you didn't get your hands broke.

"What did I tell you I was gonna do?" He asked.
"Answer me."
I obviously was terrified at this point, having seen
the extension cord in his hands where I was
expecting a paddle. He then tied my hands to the
back of the chair with another extension cord.
After I was secured and he thought I couldn't get
away, he picked up another extension cord and
then held both ends in one hand, making a "U"
shape in the cord.
"This is for not doing the dishes properly. Your
mama had to come in here and redo all these
dishes, now you're going to pay for it."
A little backstory before I continue. Yes, this was
my 7th birthday. I was forced to constantly clean
every single day from sweeping and mopping to
vacuuming, laundry, and dishes. This was the
chores I did everyday since five years old.
Today was my birthday though, and mother had
promised me an extra special gift if I did the dishes.
As a kid would I rushed through them quickly. At
one point there were so many, that I decided to just
rinse the dirty ones and that would be enough. I
was expecting my birthday gift to be given to me
immediately after I finished. Little did I know it did
not matter, as my gift wasn't coming until later.

My stepdad reared back with the extension cord,
and when it made contact with my naked back it felt
like fire had been thrown on me. The pain was so
great the second strike made me recoil and I dove
to the floor taking the chair with me.

I then crawled up underneath the table to escape the blows, using the chair in front of me as my shield.

My mother heard all the commotion from the living room, and once she saw me tied to the chair she said that all he was supposed to do was "bust my ass" and told him he'd gone too far.

She took me into the living room and smacked my rear lightly with the paddle, which of course still hurt but felt nothing like the hell I'd just endured.

She asked me if I was going to do the dishes wrong again, to which I replied no.

Meanwhile, my stepdad just didn't feel satisfied with my beating; yet knew my mom wouldn't tolerate him abusing me like that.

It was all well, I still recieved my birthday gift that day.

Just another day in paradise, they say.

4. "Welcome home"

Around some point I ended up going to second grade after enduring mother's rigorous homeschooling methods of capital punishment for failing to read properly. Needless to say, enough ass beatings taught me to read and damn good too. I was signed back into Mongolia Elementary where I had attended 1st grade a year and a half before. I quickly excelled in all my work. Even was given the offer to skip ahead to 4th grade at the end of the school year. I declined, not realizing the magnitude of my decision.
Life at home was routine at that point. If I made good grades, I didn't get beat. Pain was used as a method of making me strive to be an honor student. It was successful for the most part.
I hated failed tests, as they almost always ensured an ass beating.
Looking back on it all now, I never quite realized why my childhood was so fucked up. I guess I just never understood.

Second grade passed without a hitch, no real painful memories really stood out. Mom had this thing where she thought it was funny to tell me I could go to my grandmother's for the weekend and then not letting me go.
It was something I looked forward to every single week. I practically lived for it, and yet mom still enjoyed toying with me mentally.
That isn't to say I didn't get to go, most of the time I

did. All it would take is one wrong load of laundry, or not sweeping the floor and my whole week would be shot to hell.

I walked on eggshells all week just to see my grandmother.

Mom knew this, and that's why she thought it funny to not let me go some Friday afternoons.

Before school let out for the summer, I told all my friends farewell, as I would not be seeing them again. Mom and "Daddy" as he preferred to be called, were moving once again.

They had worked all spring to find a plot of land and a trailer to rent so that they could live in the country. New town meant new county. New county, new school. Goodbye everyone.

Moving into the trailer wasn't bad. It was nice to have three whole acres of wild open field to run around in. I loved it as a kid. My brothers and I had a blast running around playing in our new yard.

The chores continued, and the chubbiness I had as a five year old was at this point by far gone. My mother did not like me eating, except when she fed me; I sustained many beatings for sneaking food. One of those being pretzels. God, when she heard that bag rattling and came charging into the room I about pissed myself. She slapped me and took the food, as she always did.

Monster.

I was skin and bones, pale and anemic. I was only

seven at the time. Towards the end of that year I turned eight, and life in the trailer became the norm. I didn't adapt well at my new school and everyone considered me an outcast. I wasn't friendly, and at times was mean to other kids.

I remember the teacher telling me America was the greatest country in the world, to which I told her I hated America and that it wasn't the greatest country.

The whole entire class gasped and looked at me.

"Mick." Mrs. Capelin gasped, absolutely appalled. For good reason obviously, to hell with social norms and brainwashing. At least I was smart enough as a child to see that. Don't get me wrong, America is a great nation, I love being an American, but we are not the greatest in the world.

Anyway, by January that year, my brothers contracted the flu. They were all vomiting and sick with fevers. My mother decided to go shopping that night for some medicine and things to help the kids out. We stopped at Mcdonalds and my mother bought me a happy meal.

I hadn't much more gotten it scarfed down when I regurgitated.

I had thought the flu skipped me, I was the only kid in the household that hadn't contracted it yet. I knew I had been feeling off that day, but didn't expect that at all.

My mother took me directly to the hospital across from Mcdonald's at that time. I violently vomited

until I was throwing up yellow acid. I hovered over a garbage can begging for help, because I couldn't stop puking long enough to breathe.
My mom had come to care about me I guess, she tried to comfort me in my moment of need. In her own fucked up way, I guess mama always cared. The nurse came in and stuck a needle in my arm, and beyond that point I blacked out. I looked up at mom, and then my world went black.

Hours passed, and I awoke again, not realizing I had apparently some type of reaction. My grandmother was there now, crying. My mother was crying, and the whole room was full of nurses. People all around, and all I could do was crawl to the end of the hospital bed and puke in a container. I collapsed again, and that was that.
I woke up the next day being pushed along in a bed to an elevator. Mom and grandma was there with me.
I spent two whole days in the hospital before returning home. I was told I barely made it. Considering the fact that I was already a sickly little bag of bones I suppose they were right.

Everything seemed to return to normal. It wasn't until a few more months went by and I contracted the flu yet again. This time it wasn't so hard on me. Makes sense from a scientific perspective: my body was more resistant to the flu due to having contracted it before.
The first time I had it damn near killed me. The

second time though, my mom didn't sit with me in the hospital; my grandma did. She had told my grandma that she had to take me again, she couldn't keep me anymore as I nearly died the first time.

When I found out I would be going back to my grandmother's house, I was absolutely ecstatic. Nearly four years of hell was finally over.

5. "Grandma's or bust"

When mom dropped me off at grandma's I was so happy. Finally, having endured years of hell, my time had come. Free at last, free at last. It felt so good to no longer have to slave, to be able to be a kid. Something I rarely got to do.
Grandma sat on the floor with me for a moment helping me put my legos together.
She told me she loved me and got up to get her some coffee. It reminded me of the days when I was six when I'd get to visit on the weekend. She'd take me to the video store and let me rent a couple games to play on my aunt's Playstation. It was such a great time for me, as she would rent me videogames and buy me pizza from the local store. To feel loved again. To feel I could be myself. Felt like this was going to be a weekend at grandma's house forever. This was all I ever wanted and I finally had it.

After one year at grandma's, I was spoiled absolutely rotten. I ate whatever I wanted, and half the time that entailed a Digiorno's pizza and two or three Snickers followed by a bottle of gatorade. I packed on so much weight that I went from sixty five pounds to one hundred and fifty at only nine years old.
From nearly thin enough to be blown away by the wind to becoming obese. At least at this point I could fight off any more influenza, right? I was a hefty chonker let me tell you.

Spent my days firing up the Playstation and later the Playstation 2 my aunt got for christmas a few years later. Life was finally good.

If I never thanked my grandmother for loving me enough to spoil me rotten, I should have. Never did I think I would be writing this story down, only to realize how screwed up and shitty life would be for a kid to endure all that abuse.

At this point though, didn't matter anymore. I had my grandma again.

The negative repercussions of not having anymore discipline in the household became apparent after a few years however. I began to throw tantrums, I lost my temper and threw stuff. I even cussed my grandmother at one point. In short, after three years of being given anything I wanted, I was a brat.

I was obese, failing in school and had the audacity to be mean to someone who pulled me out of the wretched home life I endured for so long.

During the middle of 6th grade, my grandma decided she had had enough. I was eleven years old, and had been stealing cigarettes and not behaving. Puberty has a way with kids, turning them into pepperoni faced monsters who are impulsive as hell, and I was no exception.

My stepdad rolled into the driveway, after I got home from school. I should've expected that intro huh? Not like that had happened before or anything.

By this time, I wasn't scared of him. Or so I thought, the true lack of fear would come much later. This time though, I packed my clothes and got in the truck with him, to return to the trailer on the hill. Mom wasn't so mean anymore, she didn't care if I ate. She had her moments, but she was chilled out at this point. Not as violent either.

She knew I had been smoking, and so thought that she would punish me. What better way to punish a kid who wants to smoke, than by actually letting him smoke? Genius, right? Well, actually that's the worst thing you could do.

After having smoked a whole pack of Marlboro reds that night, I came home from school the next day and asked if I could smoke another.

Mom said yes, handed me my very own pack of Kentucky's Best Full flavors, a brand new lighter and struck a deal with me.

If I clean the house, do my chores and otherwise behave, she would buy me cigarettes.

That was a deal. From then on out, cigarettes became my life. It was all I cared about. I felt like a grown man, with my own stogie burning in my hand.

School days becoming noticeably longer with nicotine withdrawal. All I could think about was lighting a cigarette, and feel the smoke draw deep into my lungs.

Once I fell asleep in the class and was trying to smoke a pencil, to which my teacher found it amusing. "Hey Mick, you trying to roll a stogie back there?"

Guess it was obvious I smoked. Should've been, I smelled like a cigarette.

When I was still in my early addict stage, I had been smoking cigarettes probably two weeks, and I asked mom when would I know if I was addicted.

"You'll know." came her response.

She didn't like me to do it in front of people. It was supposed to be kept out of the way of others as she feared she'd be charged with child abuse. Looking back at all the shit in my life prior, buying cigarettes for a minor didn't seem like too big of a charge for her. So I said what the hell and decided to smoke at the bus stop every morning. I'd never snitch and I'd keep my smokes. Win-win, plus I thought I looked cool in front of the babes.

What teen didn't want that image? Rebellious, reckless, and misunderstood. Nothing quite says "I hate my life" like a pre-teen smoking a cigarette at the bus stop.

That's the start of a whole new chapter in my life.

6. "Seventh grade Gangsta"

School let out for the summer that year at the end of sixth grade. I was sure to end the year with a final "Fuck yeah!" before returning home to the trailer on the hill.
I made the mistake of saying something rude to a girl behind me in class, and that resulted me getting slapped by her friend and called "fatass".
Geez, you know, kids these days have it great. They get coddled and treated like a little snowflake that fell from heaven like some unique angel or something.
In my day, well, what the hell am I talking about? Abuse isn't normal. You get the point.
When I walked home from school that day, I lit a cigarette and immediately relieved myself of withdrawal symptoms. I decided that summer I was going to lift weights, that I was going to slim down and get myself in shape. I was tired of being called a fat ass, both by my "parents" and my fellow schoolmates. So I did.
Day after day that summer, I would skip meals entirely. Subsisting on nothing more than a handful of dried fruit and cigarettes.
I began doing push ups daily, and lifting weights. Trying to get big, not wanting to be weak anymore. Mom tended to help me out in that regard though, she was always making me do something. Except this time, the consequences was that she was my supplier of smokes. Failure to obey meant no smoking, so I didn't question her authority much.

My average day consisted of slave labor and cooking supper for the family. Come meal time, I'd eat half of what I'd normally eat. The intention being obvious at this point.

At night, we would play cards sometimes or my brother and I would play 'Grand Theft Auto: San Andreas' in our bedroom at the end of the trailer. The summer passed like normal.

WWE was something I had taken interest in this point. I loved watching wrestling, and even thought it was real. I looked up to the wrestlers on the television, and I wanted to be big like them. Maybe if I was big like them, nobody would pick on me.

It was also during this time I took a complete interest in becoming a future pro wrestler.

Now, what is it with people in trailers doing the same cliche shit? Watching wrestling, smoking and drinking, beating their kids, poor hygiene and eating soup from a cool whip bowl? Something about manufactured housing does that to people. In being completely honest with you though, by that point in my life I embraced the Trailerhood. I had no shame in being in a trailer. Even to this day it still feels like home to me. The school of hard knocks, in a trailer I was taught frugality. When the lights went out because mom couldn't afford to pay the bill, we made do. Mom wasn't as mean, and she became like a friend to me at this time. I actually began to feel like an adult, what with all the responsibilities in my life.

Trailer life.

At the start of that school year, I went back with a brand new attitude. I went from being a chubby outcast to a reckless and rebellious wanna be thug. I had muscle tone, grew my hair out to my neck in the classic "shaggy" fashion, and subsequently died my hair black.

I wore gold chains, sagged my pants, and listened to 'Eminem' on my portable CD player (yeah that was really old school in 2006) but I didn't care. Fuck Ipods, and fuck the rules.

That was my motto at the time. Fuck the rules. It didn't get me far to say the least.

I made lots of friends right off the bat. I was a class clown, who made it a point to back talk and rebel against authority. Passive-aggressively of course, as I still had the innate fear of physical assault. Even though teachers legally couldn't touch me, I still feared them.

It wasn't uncommon for me to throw up wrestling signs in the morning gymnasium where other kids gathered. Literally in front of everyone. The "I don't give a fuck" attitude was there. Well honed in an environment like I was raised. Other kids objected, but to hell with them. Some taunted me, but for the most part, everyone was okay with me.

Most days in seventh grade consisted of petty thuggery, me popping milk cartons in the cafeteria to impress my friends. Arm wrestling all my buddies, to show dominance, and daring out bullies that picked on smaller, weaker kids.

Our school had a 'no chains' policy for whatever

reason at the time, so for my birthday that year I asked for a chain wallet. Just to go against that standard. That wallet lasted one hour in the school before the assistant principal came in and took it from me. What point I was trying to prove exactly? Hell if I know now, but back then it was important to me.

I ended up suspended more times than I could count, and I ended up ditching school all the time. I felt I couldn't be burdened with the nonsense at school. Mom found out, and that resulted in more than a few ass beatings.

One particular day I was hiding out in the field where I had skipped school for that day. Schools called your home that day to inform you that your child was absent. Usually I tried to intercept the call, as our mom went to sleep right after we left for school. Leaving a window of opportunity to sneak back in and unplug the phone or take the automated call from school and then wipe it from the call history.
Mind you, this was the time before everybody started using cell phones entirely for their household phone. I still had the option of playing hooky without having my parents catch me, if I was quick enough.
This day though, my mom was up that morning apparently when the school called. As I said, I was

down in our field hiding out and bored to absolute shit, as I had no cell phone to entertain myself at the time.

Her voice echoed throughout the hills, let me tell you. That woman was screaming at the top of her lungs for me to get my "retarded" and "stupid" ass in the house. My heart skipped a beat, and when I went into the house I already knew what to expect. Shit, it was routine by now.

"You're gonna get your ass beat when your dad gets home." Like I haven't heard that a hundred times by now. And so it was, I was grounded; had my whole backside striped with a leather belt, from the back of my legs to my upper back, I would be whipped repeatedly.

I had begun to become immune to the pain and so sometimes I would smile after being hit. This would only infuriate my stepfather who would wail on me even harder.

He decided that belts just weren't enough. He went and got boxing gloves and decided that he was going to discipline me with those. This only made me meaner, as now I was getting used to being punched upside my head. I'd be called "retarded" to the point that it was music to my ears.

I always knew I was different, I just tried to fit in. I had an anxiety disorder that began to show around the time I turned eleven and by now it was making it harder on me to socialize in school.

This difference I had from other children, made me feel even more isolated. My mom just called me "retarded" to remind me I would never amount to anything.

I think most of how I acted at this point in my life was from all the years of physical and verbal abuse. You raise a child in a violent and abusive environment, and they become angry young men with violent tendencies. This was the case with juvenile me. I was on the border of becoming a juvenile delinquent.

I ended up suspended from school quite a lot that year. I believe I missed nearly 56 days of the entire school year between suspensions and skipping. My mom feared an investigation from child services, which she definitely deserved, but nonetheless the government failed to protect us children.

When mom would get paranoid about child services, she'd rampage, freak out, and make me clean the entire trailer top to bottom. She had a lot of these scares as we were growing up. If only she would've been a better parent I don't think she would've had anything to worry about. It's a damn shame she made sure to rob us children of our futures, at least to the best of her ability. She failed to rob me, I would later find out in life.

All hope was not lost though as I still had my cigarettes.

Summer let me out that year from my "prison" as I called it by then. It was no longer school to me, but prison. It felt like prison, the rules were so strict. My brother and I were given the mundane task that summer to cut the entire three acres of land by hand with kitchen knives. We had a plastic rubbermaid container to put the broomsage in and this proved to be a shitty task to say the least. That summer heat and lack of water damn near killed me especially after having smoked for three years at that point.

One day, my brother and I were out cutting the broomsage when my brother was playing around trying to be funny.

"Hey bub, look at me, I'm Robert." he yelled. I looked at him hunched down by a large cedar tree, looking at me.

Now Robert was a mentally ill man that lived on the other side of the fence. He wasn't a mentally competent man to say the least, and had married his mother in law. (it's Kentucky, right?)

After my brother said he was Robert, he reared back the kitchen knife above his head and stabbed it into the rubbermaid container at his legs. Either because he wasn't paying attention, or he was just being the oaf that he was, he stabbed the knife deep into his leg.

Then he pulled it out.

By the look on his face, I knew something was wrong. His eyes went blank, his mouth opened in a wide grimace. "I stabbed myself, Bub!" he yelled. Blood began pouring from his leg, dramatically. Almost like somebody turned on a water hose.

I rushed to my brother and I hoisted one arm over my shoulder to help support him. I quickly helped him hop up to the trailer from the bottom of the field.

He was pouring blood all over the ground. "It's going to be okay, Bub." I reassured him. "I've got you." Why we called each other this, I don't know. I got him onto the kitchen floor and I went and grabbed a towel. I didn't know what to do honestly, but I knew if I didn't stop the blood that I would lose my brother.

I remember reading survival manuals on idle days at my grandmother's when I was a boy. I remembered the medical skills I had read about, one particularly about bleeding.

Using that knowledge, I tied the towel just above my brother's stab wound, to "shut off" the "pipes" on his leg. I use these terms because the blood system works just like water pipes.

I then applied intense pressure above the improvised tourniquet and reassured my brother that he was going to be okay.

After several moments, I watched as the blood clotted near the wound. When I saw this, I let go of his leg and removed the tourniquet. I had saved my brother's life, I believe.

One of many to come, in the years to follow.

7. "The Panther in the hills"

Back at my grandma's when I was about ten years old. It was on a warm summer night, and quite humid. I was still living with my grandma at this time, and my mother and step dad were visiting at her house. Usually when they visited, they "borrowed" money from her. Now, when I say "borrow" I don't mean they ever paid it back. They "took" money, would be a more appropriate term, but nonetheless mom insisted it was "borrowing." As the night grew later, my parents were out on the front porch of my grandma's house. A sudden cry broke the stillness of the night. "What the fuck was that?" My mom asked.
I had been reading a book on the couch in the living room, and so I wasn't initially able to hear it. Only when my parents told me to come listen, did I know about the incident.
I stood on the porch several minutes, listening with them. Finally, after what seemed like an hour, I heard it again.
"It sounds like it's getting closer." my mother said.

"It sounds like a woman crying for help." my grandmother said. She was right, it sounded like a child or woman crying out for help. The cries broke the night, and left an eerie silence upon the land. Our dogs skimpered into their houses, afraid to come out. Something wasn't right to me.
My grandmother suggested she get her shotgun and go see where the noise was coming from. She

feared it might be the neighbors up on the hill having a fight and something was gravely wrong. The cry rang out again. It did sound like it was getting closer.

My mom and stepdad decided they were going leave. They said their goodbyes and parted, leaving my grandma and I on the porch.

At this point we called for my aunt, who was unaware of what was going on. She came out, and eventually heard the noise too. She went into the house and returned with a hunting knife in her hand.

My grandmother went and fetched her father's old break barrel single-shot shotgun he had left her, and loaded birdshot into the breach.

She lay the old scattergun across her lap as she sat on the swing. We listened for several moments, and heard absolutely nothing. I being the dumb kid I was, went and got a claw hammer from the hallway where my grandpa kept his tools. I wanted to help too, and apparently I had to be armed to do so.

My grandma chuckled at the sight of me on the porch with her, and a claw hammer in my hand. I was just a little boy, and I knew something we didn't understand was lurking in the woods nearby. I wanted to protect her, even if I was chunky and 4'11. That was my granny.

After half an hour, and hearing absolutely nothing, I began to think nothing was going to happen. My grandma had given me a large spotlight to scan around the yard with, as most of her yard was rural, forested and very dark.

My grandpa came home and was standing by the porch on the ground, leaning against the rail. He quickly dismissed what we were claiming.

We had no clue what this noise was, or what it belonged to. My god, it was terrifying to say the least.

The foreboding stillness was still upon the yard, no dog we had dared bark or move. They were alert, with their eyes peering out of their houses from me reflecting the light off their eyes.

I had learned at a young age at night to watch where our dogs were looking to determine what it was they were alerting me to. So I was trying to see if they were looking anywhere in the yard. I knew they would be able to see it.

At this point, the dogs were just looking at me. Grandpa and grandma continued talking, while I scanned the yard with the spotlight. During a break in their conversation I heard a very distinct sound of a twig breaking under heavy weight by a large tree in the dark part of our yard. Just out of reach of the security light.

I shone the light immediately in the direction. I was horrified.

I began to have trouble speaking. "Eyes." was all I could choke out to my grandma. She could tell I lost all color in my face.

There, where the noise came from, were orange eyes about two and a half feet off of the ground. I

could see nothing else, just the eyes.
At first my grandma didn't see it, but when she did, she shot down the porch steps and walked towards the creature with scattergun in hand. She crouched down, and placed the stock of the gun to her shoulder. I had kept the light on the eyes, so that she could see her target. The eyes couldn't have been no further than 20 yards from us. They were really close. I saw the eyes recoil when my grandmother fired. The shot sounding like the loudest thunder you've ever heard as it broke the sound barrier, and the stillness of the night.

The blast made my aunt rush outside to see what was going on, as she had returned inside prior seeing the earlier incident as uneventful. Something ran through our woods, just shortly after the shot, and then silence returned to the night. My grandpa took the spotlight from me, and we all filed into a line before searching the yard. Grandpa with the flashlight, grandma with the shotgun, my aunt with her hunting knife, and I with my hammer (a force to be reckoned with at the time, lol.) scanned the dark yard for any sign of the creature. Our search proved to no avail and we soon stopped looking after that.
The next day, my grandmother went to work where she was a cook at our local family restaurant in our small town. She told the people there about the crying in the middle of the night. An avid hunter there told her that people had seen cougars in our area at the time. One of the men told my grandma

that what she encountered was a "house cat" in
heat. My grandma recoiled at the idea, reassuring
him that despite his mansplaining, what she
encountered was solid black as it had to have been
to not be seen by our bright spotlight.

Nobody believed her, except the man who
confirmed cougars were in the area at the time.
That was unusual as cougars were not in our part
of the state usually.
Mind you, this was the state of Kentucky. We do
not have any large cats in the part of Kentucky I
was raised in, thereby making the experience all
the more fascinating, and terrifying to my childlike
imagination.
The joke turned around quickly on the mind as one
of the men from the restaurant who had been
laughing at my grandmother was driving home
down the country road a mile from my grandma's
house, when a large black cat shot across the road.
The size of it shook the man up immensely. My
grandma told them she had seen it. I didn't
understand shotguns at the time, so I was confused
as to how my grandmother hadn't killed it.
She later told me she didn't aim at the animal, in
case of it being a neighbor's dog, but rather shot to
the right of it to scare it.
Looking back, had she hit it, the poor thing
would've been blind as she was just using birdshot,
a rabbit load for a 20 gauge. Therefore, the animal
would've been maimed and blinded for the rest of
its life at best. That's why my grandma didn't aim at

it.

For those of you who don't know what birdshot is, it's hundreds of tiny lead pellets than travel well over 1250 fps. Ouch. They are only lethal to large game and humans at very close range.

She came home from work that day and told us that somebody at the restaurant had seen the cat too. It was without question at this point to all of us: there was something in the woods.

8. "Eighth grade manhood"

Towards the end of summer in seventh grade, I still
kept up my shenanigans of being a rebellious thug
with no real friends. There was reasons to why I did
it, to me at the time, violence was an acceptable
resolution to problems. Violence solved issues
between each other.
My brother and I beat the hell out of each other,
alot.
Now that I'm older, and grown "soft", I am sorry for
what I did. I apologized to my brother so many
times. He didn't deserve any of that. I didn't
deserve all the ass kickings we gave each other
either.
We both had hard lives, that should've made us
stronger in our bond. We were the outcasts of the
family, and so it was important for the two of us to
stick together.
I, however, didn't like my brother at the time
because he was a troublemaker. Ironically, I
couldn't see I was too.

One particular day, my brother (who was 13) had
"borrowed" small bottles of vodka from some
bootlegger in our small town. Bootleggers were
necessary in our county at the time as alcohol was
prohibited, and so to get booze you'd have to drive
a long way.
Back to the story, my brother got absolutely shit
faced drunk, something our mother didn't mind us
doing so long as we didn't get caught. He ran up

and down our street butt ass naked screaming his name to hell and all of Kentucky.
This my mother found hilarious, as she always found him funny. Admittedly, this was normal behavior to me so I found it funny too. My brother was always trying to make people laugh; To make friends, and he was good at it.
This was our life at this point. "Bub" now smoked cigarettes too. We were both hooked on smokes. Mom's motto was "she'd rather us do it at home, than to do it with random strangers."
So cigarettes and alcohol were okay in her book, regardless of our age. Just as long as we were safe and sound at home.

When school began again in the fall of 2007, I started eighth grade. I was expecting it to be a complete walk in the park like the year prior. I thought I'd walk in, make a shit ton of friends, and walk out like a boss.
To me, it wasn't the start of a new school year for me. It was the return to greatness, just like in the WWE when a wrestler took a hiatus and then made his debut again. I yearned for the fame I had the year prior, and thought I'd be greeted with people who were happy to see me again.
To my suprise, upon entering the gymnasium, nobody was happy to see "that kid" again. I had gotten new "threads" from Old Navy and was excited to be "fly" in front of the ladies.
I hadn't been in school 15 minutes and already gave away my leather spiked bracelet I was

wearing in an attempt to make a friend. I was a "yes man" back then and so I would give you anything you asked for and not say no, just because I wanted to make a friend.
What an idiot.

Ended up finding out that all my friends I had the year before had been separated from me. We all shared the same grade, but we had been divided in "teams" which is to say: that people on one team attended classes at a different time than the other team. All my friends were placed on a different team. All the rowdy guys I was raising hell in class with the year prior and been handpicked to be put on a team opposite of me. It was an attempt by the teachers the year prior who had several problems with me, to isolate me; maybe then I would behave. Mainly because I believe they saw I was merely a follower, and not the leader I thought I was: and I acted out to impress my friends.
Separate me from them, and I would be less likely to act out. They were exactly right. They made one mistake though, I still had one friend who never acted out with me but we had been best friends since the third grade. His name was William. He preferred the name "Willy" and therefore our friendship began.
Willy and I had one Tech Ed class together where we could see each other and hang out. It was the only time of the day I looked forward to as most of the school year had passed and I had failed to make any real friends.

Most of my school day consisted of sitting silently in class, not interacting with anyone. Guess the teachers before were right in isolating me- and it worked for the most part.

When I got to see Willy, we would laugh and crack jokes. We'd always talk and hang out. He was a cool guy, at least by my standards. In reality he was on the nerdy side, and I was a "gangsta" but I liked Willy all the same.

One day Willy and I had a disagreement, and he got an attitude with me. Coming from the background of violence I did, to argue with me was disrespecting me. To disrespect me meant we had to settle it with violence.

Willy was not a fighter, under no circumstances. He was a very "mama's boy" type of person. He also had mild seizures occasionally during school, and it's because of this I would sometimes mock him seizing up to make him laugh. Willy didn't like this and so asked me to stop. I apologized at my attempt to make light of a serious situation. I only did so because Willy was really embarrassed of holding his hands in the air and jerking whenever he'd have a fit. I being his friend, was trying to be a comic relief. It failed, and hurt Willy's feelings.

I told Willy I didn't appreciate the tone he was using with me, and told him he "Didn't want none." So that was the end of that friendship. We stopped talking after that.

Having been threatened with being placed in a school for bad kids, where they were incredibly strict, I began to walk on eggshells around the school. I'd been accused of doing things this time, that I hadn't actually done. Someone told somebody that I had, and it's that very hearsay that was required to "convict" me as I called it, to in-school-suspension. It was basically a tiny room where you were locked in with other kids for the whole of the day. No windows, no nothing. Just school work, and silence. We weren't allowed to talk and it was basically like segregation that they used in modern prison.

To an eighth grader, it was hell on earth. I had to go sit in "Ad-seg" and go through nicotine withdrawal at the same time.

Well, as usual, somebody said I harassed someone in the halls, and so I ended up spending three entire days in "Ad-seg". The song I related to during those days was called "Locked up" by Akon. It literally felt like I was in prison. You didn't feel human in "Ad-seg" and I'm not sure if kids today still have to go through it. It really goes without saying that if you get known for doing something, it's easier to convict you when you're innocent. All I can say is, I did my time; but I didn't do the crime.

During all this time, my brother had also started to go to middle school with me. He was a sixth grader, and just like myself, prone to mischief.

The only highlight of my year other than constantly being suspended, or otherwise just laying low awaiting my next suspension, was my brother getting picked on by a school bully. I caught wind of this, and found the three guys who had been bullying my brother and taking his food.

There they sat, three large kids sitting at a table in the cafeteria. By this point, I was going to be suspended for something anyway, might as well be actually guilty for once. I approached the three kids, and dared the biggest one out. I called him "A motherfucker" and threatened to knock all three of their teeth out if they fucked with my little brother again. I assured them that If they decided to "jump" that this frog was ready. I was ready to lay the first one out if he stood up to attack me. It was three against one, so I knew I had to clip chins quick with my fists if I were to succeed.

Needless to say, these big dudes clammed up. Nobody said a thing, but I made sure they knew the name of their victim. I let them know why I was ready to fight and I let them know if they did it again, there would be consequences.

My brother finally could eat his food in peace, and nobody fucked with him again at that point. My job was done.

We had run-ins, my brother would always tell me if someone was bothering him, and I'd confront the bully. My brother was a big baby, and not a fighter by any means. I loved him, and I had an honor code to my family. I always dealt with the problems accordingly. Most of the time, it never took more than a warning. Nothing ever became physical, as I was known for being the "crazy kid" with a quick temper.

Once on the bus ride going home, a kid threw gum in my hair. Now, my hair was long, about down to my neck and I loved it dearly. Having gum matted in it set off my "bipolar rage" which made me jump up and confront the whole entire bus.

I screamed at everyone and asked them "who the fuck did it? Which one of you motherfuckers saw who did?" and nobody confessed. The kid sitting behind me was known as a little smart aleck and known for making trouble. I immediately suspected him as he'd been chewing the same colored gum earlier but now wasn't.

"Did you do it?!" I yelled. "I don't know what you're talking about." he replied sarcastically. I reared back my fist resisting the urge to punch him in the face, he hunkered down and apologized. Still he didn't admit to it. I called everyone a "cocksucker" and sat back down, satisfied I had proven my point. Now, it seems like the person I had become was like that of an inmate. It's strange how human beings become a product of their environment. Even more so how pain makes a person stronger. The person I had become from living with my family was not the person I would be later in life, I found. However, it was necessary for survival in the environment I was in. I felt like an animal, and was treated like one, so my logic was, "Why not be one?" and so I was.

I made friends during this year with a kid named Ryan, who I had known in elementary school as someone who bullied me. He started picking on my brother. Taking my brother's shoelaces out of his shoes and tossing them out the window. My brother got those custom shoelaces for school, and really loved them. Ryan had also told everyone about my brother's bed wetting problem. Further making my brother humiliated as the back of the bus broke out in laughter, calling my brother "pissy pants".

Sure enough, my brother ran from the back of the bus and told me about it. Hearing this, and seeing my little brother crying, I calmly took my headphones off. I placed my CD player in my backpack, zipped it up, and got out of my seat. The look on Ryan's face as I approached him went from cocky, to his eyes widening.

"You picking on my brother?" I asked quietly. The whole bus went quiet, all eyes on me. "No." Ryan said.

Within a split second, I punched him in the face and the force sent him toppling over into the seat. I guess the bus driver never noticed or pretended not to, because she never said anything about this.

"That's a warning. If I hear about this shit again, we're going to have even more problems." He said nothing. I returned to my seat and placed my headphones on. That was all it took to start the next events.

A couple weeks later, Ryan had been hanging out with my brother. They quickly became friends. I had hung out with the kid but didn't like him that much. As usual bus rides go, today would change the course of this history. My brother still insisted on being at the back of the bus, trying to make friends with the scum that hung out back there. Ryan was now joking around with my brother too.

A big kid, who was a football player in our school, had taken offence to something my brother was talking about.

Mind you I was 5'10 at this time, this big kid was 6'1 and outweighed me by nearly 90 lbs.

I was at the front of the bus listening to music on my headphones, when I saw my brother run past me towards the front of the bus. "Bub!" was all he got out. I looked behind him, and this big kid was barreling down the aisle towards him.

Ryan had been caught between the two, and thought the kid was after him.

I came up out of my seat, with a "The fuck you are." as the kid had roared he was going to "Kick your ass." at my little brother.

I stood face to face with this giant. Looking him in the eye, and prepared to do extreme violence. I stopped his charge in his tracks, as I stood between him and my little brother. I didn't break eye contact with him. His tone changed, "I don't wanna fight you man." "There ain't gonna be a fight." I said. I meant it in the sense that I was going to knock him unconscious before he could overpower me.

My brother began screaming at the big kid with, "My brother will kick your ass. You don't want to fuck with him."

"Bub, shut the fuck up and sit down." I said, turning my head to face him for a second.

My brother shut up. "Now," I said calmly, "There's not going to be any fight."
"Tell your brother to keep his fucking mouth shut." the kid replied. "I'm not telling him shit, just forget this shit happened." I responded. I remember looking back at the whole bus looking at this giant kid, and looking at me.
The girl I had a crush on at the time was smiling at me, like she was proud of me or someshit. I kept cool, and de escalated the whole situation.
After the kid sat back down, I heard his buddy say "I had your back."

Ryan, shaken up by what had just happened, looked at me and thanked me. "For what?" I thought. I never asked.
All I know is that we all three became best friends after that.

9. "Sleeping under the stars"

While school life died down, I settled in. I still remained an outcast, it was cool with me though. My brother stopped having problems altogether with people picking on him. Ryan, "Bub" and I all planned on going camping in the woods near my grandmother's house. This was something I had dreamed about from a very young age. I always wanted to go camping but was too afraid to do it alone.

Hell, who wouldn't have been with the "panther" scare.

We got off the bus at our house that day, and went and rode with our mother to the store. We bought the tent, sodas, canned food and some hot dogs. We were so excited to go out in the woods for the weekend.

To be free of all the burdens and slavery that my weekends usually entailed, I loved having my friend over since that seemed to make my family bother me less. My mother had an image to maintain, and my stepdad whined and complained but that was about it.

We quickly headed out that cool Friday afternoon. It was early autumn and so was chilly enough to need some proper clothing, yet as I always did like the winters before, I wore only a t-shirt.

I brought along a couple spare packs of cigarettes, as all three of us smoked. We placed high priority over food, our smokes.

We sat up the tent, and started a fire. We watched as the sun went down. There we were, under the stars. Wild. Free. Coyotes howling in the distance. For the first time in a while I felt like I was in touch with what it meant to be human.

We spent the whole weekend smoking, eating and just living. We talked, I read books, my brother went back to my grandma's house to eat. We wasn't far away but the walk did take 20 minutes through the cow pastures to get back to the road and to my grandmother's house.

When the weekend ended, I felt sad. Knowing I had to return to society and be a good pupil.

First thing that Monday, Ryan and I were talking about doing it all again. We loved the woods, and yearned to go back. That didn't happen for weeks later, and by now it was late autumn. We tried to camp again but it was never the same. The first night, it rained. Our tent became flooded inside, and we awoke cold and wet. We hadn't went back to the same place that night, but attempted it right near our trailer instead, by the fence row and in tall grass.

We awoke in the dark absolutely drenched. Mad dashes in the pouring down rain ensued. We all three was making way for the trailer. When we stripped ourselves of our wet clothes, it felt so good to be warm and cozy; we all fell asleep shortly thereafter.

Our mom gave us a ride to our grandma's house and we decided to go back to our original camping spot. My idea was so I could experience what I had before.

As I said though, cold and wet wasn't exactly a great experience, and so we quit the camping trip that weekend and returned home. Vowing to give it another go one day soon.

Another few weeks dragged on, we decided to give it another go. Sad to say, while the weather allowed us to camp. It was never the same, and the creek nearby had flooded due to recent rains, covering our old spot.

We spent the weekend on a small area of ground, by the water. Overlooking the field that had now become a lake, as it always does nowadays during heavy rain.

Our tent broke, and we were unable to get it put up to sleep in. Instead, we just stretched it out on the ground and laid atop it. It wasn't supposed to rain to our knowledge despite Kentucky weather being known to change on a dime.

That night, when it came time to bed down, Bub and Ryan went into the collapsed tent on the ground to sleep. I had already drifted off to sleep by the fire, and that's where I remained until morning, under the stars.

The rest of the camping trip resulted in good times, one of those being my brother shit himself. Ryan and I had a good laugh at that.

Just old Bub shenanigans.

As I sat talking to Ryan, I heard a splash way across the water. Ever so faint, and towards the base of where the stream would've been, at the bottom of a rockstrewn hill.

A large black animal, about the size of a dog, drinking from the water. It then turned slowly and retreated up over the hill.

"The black panther." I thought. I then told Ryan the story of when I was younger, and explained what I had seen. He didn't seem to believe me.

I guess it did seem a little far fetched, and while that black thing could've been a dog or anything but a black cougar, I still felt like it very well could have been.

To this day I still think it was. That was the last time I've ever seen another black cougar or anything like it in the hollers of Kentucky though.

10. "Something to prove"

Ryan was over one night, and it was towards the end of the 8th grade school year. I had been drinking whiskey and Ryan came off with something smart to say, which resulted in me threatening to fight him. Thus abruptly ending our friendship.
Now, Ryan opened my bedroom window, hopped out and told me to go "Fuck myself." That was that. So long ol chum.

I finished my days in middle school without Ryan, and deep within I found a resonating sadness deep in my heart. Knowing that I was off to high school, and would not see any of my old friends again. This was bittersweet, as school was out for the summer. I had nothing to look forward too except a whole two months of getting punched by my stepdad every time I stepped out of line. When the bus took me away, I looked back one last time that day, at all that I had seen before and taken for granted. I reminisced on all the times I had at school. Both good and bad. The more I thought of the bad though, the happier I became to say fuck that place.
It was during this summer that I worked at our local family owned diner as a busboy. I did this under the table for 80.00 a week. I used that money to buy cigarettes and eat Chinese buffet once a week. Not a bad trade off, and I felt like an adult.

It so happened one night that a couple kids hanging out back behind the restaurant were loitering. I was told to go tell them to leave, since they were my age. I did tell them to leave, introduced myself and was respectful in asking them to go. They obliged and left.

Weeks later, I'm out back behind the trailer in the dead of night, around 8 or 9pm. My stepdad was home, and my mother was out buying groceries or something, just know she wasn't there.
I'm blasting my music on speakers I have pulled out my bedroom window, and drinking whiskey. I'm half ass dancing and just having a big one man party to myself.
The two kids I met at the restaurant showed up. Little did I know they're had been word on the street that they wanted to kick my ass. So here they were, smiling and laughing, one waiting for the other to swing. They never did, and at fourteen almost fifteen, I was the oldest. I offered both of them some whisky. Before you knew it, we were all dancing and acting fools. We threw some kind of sausage fest by only being guys hanging out, but that's back before people had a term for it. To us, it was a party. These guys checked out, they were alright in my book. We all partied well into the night, and then when my mom came home, my new friends (We'll call one Chance and the other Robert because I don't want them reading this) and I were all in the living room partying. My stepdad soon got drunk and started dancing too. That shit was

awkward as I'd never seen the rat ever dance. He was always beating us kids with his fists and yelling. He was never happy (well, he stopped beating me by then but I'll explain later).
At one point Chance was walking around outside and actually managed to fall off the porch. We all found this hilarious.
We all passed out hours later, between puking and drinking more. Those guys didn't go home until the next day.

I returned to work at the restaurant in the days to follow. The guys used to hang out with me on break. They'd bum smokes and we'd all sit and talk about life. Talking about hanging out after work, talk about girls. Alot about girls actually. Hell, between that and getting laid, we never shut the fuck up about it. That's what teenage boys do. All you can think about is that sweet nectar and then once you get it, it wasn't worth all you had to do to get it.
Flash forward into the future, Robert was talking dirty about my little sister. I found out through a cell phone text while eating my chicken snack wraps from McDonald's.
This upset me majorly. My little sister was like 4 or 5 at the time. I get home that day, walk to a local friends house and lure Robert to the house under the ruse that my little brother wanted to fight him. He obliged immediately, knowing my brother was known as the town punching bag.
When he went in the private area that was the back yard, I proceeded to beat the ever living shit out of

Robert. I told him to not every mention my baby sister again. This set the stage of my betrayal almost 5 months to come.

This guy I thought was my friend turned out to be a snake. He wasn't worthy to lick the bottom of my shoe in my eyes. We end up not hanging out for a good long while. I happen to be walking to get some cigarettes from a guy I knew sold them to minors, when there was a commotion in the old ball park. I saw people and vehicles every damn where. A bunch of guys and some pretty ladies, so I thought, alright. I'm checking this shit out. I began asking around about what was this commotion about. A guy told me a girl had been talking trash about another girl and other drama. I was informed there was going to be a fight, so I hung around. This girl rolls up on the scene, hops out and starts swinging on this girl that I was just talking to. They're going at it, ass cracks hanging out, hair flying.
One of the young teenage girls sees that her mama is getting beat down, so she grabs a baseball bat out of the back of the truck and approaches the woman and tells her to get off her mom. The woman didn't much more say "Or what?" before I heard the loud ringing of the bat against her skull. That woman was sprawled all over the concrete. She lay dead still.
That little girl is dangerous. I thought I had just witnessed a murder and the way she started swinging at everybody I thought I was next. That

bitch was crazy.

Everyone began driving off and fleeing the scene. I took off in a dead sprint up the hill towards home. Some of the guys offered me a ride and I hopped in the car and we got the fuck out of there.

It wasn't until a few days later I found out the woman was alright. She had a severe head injury and suffered a concussion, but otherwise was stable. She was talking to Robert and I as it was his distant cousin or something.

If I had a cell phone I would've called the police, but this was a time when cell phones weren't very common. I was poor white trash, I could barely afford my own smokes at the time, let alone a phone bill.

Anyways, I found out the crazy girl got charged with attempted murder and aggravated assault. I've heard nothing of it to this day. Back then though, shit like this was everyday in my town.

Full of meth heads, crack hoes, and white trash. It was what I called home. I thought I was king of the hill, that I had nothing to fear. I was wrong.

Now then, You might be wondering why the hell I was hanging out with Robert again. If you asked me that now, I'd tell you because I was a dumbass. If you asked me that back then, I'd tell you because he apologized and told me that he never said that about my sister, and that it was Chance who said it. Why I believed him? I don't know. All I know is that Chance found out I was after him and he steered clear of me. We never spoke to him again.

At the end of summer, my mother decided she couldn't legally sign me out of school, so instead was going to "homeschool" me, by basically dropping me out of school, saying I was being taught, but me not actually doing any school work. I ended up never seeing my classmates from middle school.
That happened about a year later after these next few events.
Winter came, I wasn't in school while the rest of the kids I had known was, and by then I was already fifteen. It's in January, right after christmas, when this big ice storm of 2009 hits Kentucky. We lost power in the trailer for nearly two weeks, the power was completely gone. People all over the state was freezing and without power. It made news headlines, it was a national crisis. A Lot of people died from the cold, and I was lucky to have survived.

Robert and I spent the next few days trying to keep warm, I would be off roaming my home town and looking for ways to keep warm. I checked on elderly people I knew, and kept them company for some time. It was an absolute mess. Robert suggested we go stay in a town way south called "Cave city" that still happened to have power in some areas. My parents, siblings and step dad's brother all went to a motel in Cave city and that's where the next part of this story happens.
My family all stayed at the motel, whilst I insisted on

hanging out with the snake that was Robert.

I didn't know that the city I was in had a high crime rate, much worse than my small town.

Robert had family that lived down there in one of the motels. I'm not sure how that was allowed, but the mother knew the owner quite well and I'm assuming that's why. That, and she worked there. Anyway, his family knew I had attacked Robert, and they set me up. A big guy they knew picked me up by the neck without warning and proceeded to choke the ever loving shit right out of me. He was a big man, standing well around 6'9 and weighed god only knows how much. I weighed only 150 lbs, and stood barefoot at 5'10. I was no match for this guy, and he knew it. He manhandled me like a stuffed animal. At one point he pushed me into the corner asking me "What are you gonna do now?" and I replied with a hard push that knocked him off balance.

Bipolar rage had set in, and it at least made me way stronger than I normally was. Kind of like adrenaline, but still no match for a full on fight with this guy. I wasn't scared of him, I just didn't want to have any beef with anyone at the time, he was Robert's friend.

Meanwhile, all this shit is going on, Robert's sitting in the corner laughing. Some friend.

I stopped hanging around Robert that day. I decided he was a snake and I deserved the bite I got for picking him up. He never did see me again after that. I went back to the motel and stayed there

with my family until the electricity was restored and
then we returned to the trailer on the hill.
My pride was hurt. Should've known then I couldn't
win every fight, but I was young.

11. "New beginnings"

I've always kept my whole life in a suitcase. This is
something I've known since my childhood. I
bounced from home to home, back and forth nearly
all my life.
 It became against my very nature to settle down in
one place, and to this day I still do not want to
settle. I yearn to travel, as I suffer with a condition
known as wanderlust.
It drives you onward, almost maddened to the brink
of new horizons.
In February of 2009, I was no different. I awoke to
the sound of my biological grandfather's voice in
the kitchen.
My grandmother Bonnie, who had been battling
terminal lung cancer, passed away. He had come
down to see if I would like to attend to her funeral.
I, being the dumb young punk who at this point did
not give two shits about anybody or anything,
agreed.
He told me that my grandmother had died.
"About damn time." I said.
It was not called for, and highly disrespectful. I
regret that I had said that. I didn't know my
biological grandfather's wife, Bonnie. As she wasn't
my actual grandmother. Still, no need to be such a
punk to my grandfather.
He gave me a ride to Shepherdsville that day,
where my family from my father's side originated. I
saw long lost faces who had only been a blur to
me. My uncles, my cousins, my aunts. All the

people who I had seen as a young boy on visits, but had never seen again until now that I was halfway to twenty.

Everyone acted happy to see me, but everything quickly turned to my late grandmother's funeral.

I attended visitation for the day, and as they brought my father into the funeral home, I quickly clammed up.

This was the man that my mother hated me because of. She always said I looked like him, that I was "retarded" like him, that I was a piece of shit, just like him.

There he stood and I saw the resemblance. My god, I did look just like him. Without a doubt, that was my father. I didn't realize that the man had severe mental problems, and was unable to halfway communicate with people. What the actual fuck did my mom see in this guy? What the fuck mom? This guy had special problems, and here I was unable to shake his hand despite everybody in the family trying to get me to talk to him.

This was the man that "abandoned" my mom and me for a cheap hooker at the local Shepherdsville truck stop. This was the man that I was hated for? But he was harmless. Why was I hated because of being his son exactly? Nothing made any sense to me. This didn't make any sense. My anxiety acted up and I began to become really tense. My uncle Terry was sitting at the table with me, and he and I had gotten along pretty well. He was a down to earth guy.

He saw that I was having an emotional breakdown right in front of everyone and asked me if I would like to go for a ride. I obliged and we left the funeral home.

He took me back to the apartment, and left me there to compose myself. I was really shaken up from the incident. I faintly remember my father a long time ago and remembered him as an angry man. I had visited him around six when he was still with his old wife. He was mean to me, and began cursing and screaming at me and I became very frightened. The plan was to stay the night with them but I ended up back at my grandmother Bonnie's house that night, where I remained for the rest of the weekend.

Bonnie told my mother she did not want me back up there, that she did not want me there period and that was that.

Now, all this shit was making sense to me. It all began adding up.

My mother actually loved my father, but he cheated on her while she was 8 months pregnant with me. He broke her heart and she was madly in love with him. That's why she resented me. I reminded her of the love she lost, and she felt she wasn't good enough. I reminded her of her inadequacy, and her "could have been" husband.

She claims it's because she hated him, but you have to love someone dearly in order to hate them with such intensity.

It all made sense. All the puzzle pieces finally fit

into place.

Weeks go by, I had settled into the apartment with my grandfather and we begin to live together. I didn't have school to worry about, and I much loved the new city I was in. I was happy where I was at and I remained there for well over 6 months. It was around July before I ended up leaving Shepherdsville.
During that time I had discovered the internet and all its glory. I would sneak onto my grandpa's computer and watch youtube videos all day while he worked the ten hour shift.
I loved paranormal stuff and was such a sucker for it I believed any supposed ghost video I watched. From stop animated army men, to proof of god, to ouija board videos. I absorbed it like a sponge.

I began to study Wicca, and wanted to learn witchcraft. I truly believed in this stuff at the time, and believed spells would work. I bounced from one subject of the occult to the other, from satanic chants to spells for wicca.

I knew my grandmother had passed away in that very apartment and so I wanted to obtain a Ouija board and commune with the dead.

This was problematic, because I was 15, had no job, and no money. Where the hell was I going to come up with twenty dollars?

My mom came up that day, bringing me some chewing tobacco (as I had quit smoking by now) and some groceries. She would visit with me, and we'd talk about stuff. She'd spend most of her time talking on the phone and smoking cigarettes. As was typical of her at home.

Mom decided she'd buy it for me, and she gave me a ride up to Louisville to the local "Toys-R-US" and I found a glow in the dark Ouija board.

I went home and immediately toyed with it. Nothing happened. This didn't dishearten me immediately. In the bedroom drawer it went until I decided to do something with it.

A few weeks later, I'm in the living room and home alone again, as was routine by now. I decided to bust out the Ouija for old time's sake. This was a terrible idea on my behalf, though I didn't realize it. I tried to get the board to work again, but to no avail. I decided I was gonna do everything I was told not to do with the board. I began making a figure eight on the board using the planchette, all the while repeatedly chanting:

"Archangel. Dark Angel.
Lend me thy light.
Death's veil
Until we have heaven in sight."

I had learned this from a Youtube video, and didn't think any of this was legitimate. At one point, I saw movement in the corner of my eye while I was chanting this. It was tall and shadowy, and it's clothing was as black as it but flowy, like a robe. By the time I looked to the right of me to see what this was, it was gone.
As I was looking at where it was, a dramatic pause happened, and then I saw the picture frame fall. I cried out in fear, broke the board and tossed it in the trash. I was terrified.
To this day, I know that the shit I experienced with the Ouija board was real, and I have never touched it again. You invite things in your house that don't belong there.

By the end of July, I had grown tired of the city, and of all my ghost hunting escapades, and decided to return to my grandmother's rural home back in my hometown. My biological grandfather hated to see me go, whether he admitted it or not. I had an argument with my mother and I told her I will not be coming back to her house. I didn't want to live there.

She told me I could go live with my grandmother again, and so I thought about the last time I had lived there, I was eleven or so. It would be a new experience.
After packing my belongings, I called for my grandmother and she came and got me.

That was that, I was gone from Shepherdsville forever.

At least for a few years, anyway.

72

- 12. "Dropping out"

By the time I even went to high school, after several failed attempts for me to attend the local adult education center, I dropped out within the first four months. What the hell was the point of me even going, you ask? My mother thought that it would relieve her of having to come up with an excuse to tell the school board about why the hell I wasn't in school.

Now, I show up to the high school right before the year started, to enroll in what I thought was going to be the tenth grade. I show up with my mother, we go and sit in the principal's office and do what I'll call an "interview" as that's the best way I can describe it.

It wasn't like usual, they asked me what I had completed the year prior, home school wise.

I told them I had went through a program called "Lifeway" which was true, because my mother bought the homeschool books from the local christian bookstore.

This did not satisfy the principal in the slightest. He asked me what it was I studied.

"History, Language Arts, Math, Science, and Bible." I replied.

Apparently "Bible" isn't a school subject,

and so he threw my ass into the 9th grade. Mind you, this was the same school where my friends from the middle school prior were at. By this time, a year had passed since eighth grade and so all my friends were sophomores by now. I didn't want to be a freshman.

I got disheartened, but really it was my fault to showing up at the interview with a gigantic cross necklace dangling from a large metal chain around my neck. I looked retarded. Hell, at this point I was asking to be laughed at.

Still, I was just me at the time, and didn't mind if people laughed at me for being a devout christian, as this was considered a blessing to be "picked on for Jesus" in my eyes.

A form of persecution, a favorable tribulation in the eyes of the Lord.

Having enrolled in high school, and knowing there was a good chance I would never see any of my old friends again, I prepared for the worst and began watching the days tick by before school started. This was gonna be a complete nightmare.

Social anxiety was something that always plagued me as a child. I was always this really quiet, awkward kid who didn't know how to interact with the world. I ended up worrying to the point my stomach would

hurt, either because of the trauma I had suffered or the chaotic and unstable environment I was brought up in, I worried about everything, every single hour of the day.
Teenage years being no exception.
So of course I was worrying about school.
New faces, new image, nobody knew me.
Either I could reinvent myself, or try my old tactics to fit in.
If it's not broke don't fix it.

The summer draws to an end, the school year finally starts after all of my anticipation. The very night before school I kneeled at the edge of the couch where I slept and said a prayer that I might have strength the following day. Prayed that I would be strong enough to face the challenges to come. That I would fit in.
I awoke the next day around 7am and quickly rushed to get ready. I thought I was going to miss the bus, and so I skipped showering and brushing my teeth and just ran out to the end of my grandma's driveway.
There, I waited in the cool morning for a bus to come.
And waited some more.
No bus, still I waited.
I stood in the morning chill, spitting tobacco juice and waiting eagerly; still nothing.

That's when mom comes driving by, telling me to get in. Apparently I had already missed the bus. Real smart, I felt like an idiot.
Now I was gonna look like one too with my mom driving me to school at almost 16.
I was a man, damnit. At least I thought anyway.
Realistically my real manhood wouldn't come for several more years down the road, when I would experience the real challenges of life. I was just wet behind the ears right now, but I thought I knew it all.

Mom rolls up at the school an hour later, as she had to drive me from the rural parts where I lived to the city of the school, over 30 miles away.
I get out, and go into the office absolutely embarrassed. As I walked by the cafeteria, the amount of other kids in there was overwhelming. There were thousands, literally thousands of people. I felt my chest tighten. I couldn't breathe. I was choking and I hadn't even started yet.
It was these exact feelings that I felt every single day of high school. I didn't even understand why I felt them, I just knew that they were happening. That I wasn't normal, I was sure. I felt like a freak, and all I wanted to do was blend in to the crowd. I filed into the mass of kids in the hall and

slowly made my way to class, where my day
dragged on from there.

Every social interaction was me, raspy
voiced and choking on words, unable to
communicate with my fellow freshmen. I felt
awkward being a year older than these kids.
I stood out too, because I was much taller
than most of them. Not everybody had
made it to 5'11 which was now the height I
stood, having grown more over the past
year.

I towered over a lot of these kids, and I
looked almost like an 18 year old kid.

Eventually, I found that I could ditch certain
classes. The logic behind this was that while
teachers called for attendance every single
class. If I ditched the very first class of the
day, I could choose what classes to show
up for, and just claim to have been late.
Teachers never check that out, and so
seemed like a plan. I didn't particularly like
gym class either, and was the main class I
feared most. It required me to open up and
come out of my shell, and I just tried so hard
to blend in. Gym didn't allow concealment. It
all too often had me exercise awkwardly in
front of other kids, so I decided I would ditch
it.

A little backstory before I continue, you
might be asking why I didn't just skip school

those days altogether. The answer to that is my grandmother 'made' me go to school. If I skipped class, my mom found out about it, and she threw a fit on me for it.

If my grandmother caught me skipping school, she would go stand outside and scream my name at the top of her lungs until I would show up.

Luckily my grandmother had still worked at the local restaurant my family owned. She worked the day shift, and so I saw how I could play that in my favor.

Now, schools still called home during this time to inform parents that you were not in school. My grandmother's house number was on the contact phone, and so I knew chances were she'd be gone long before they called her. I was right.

My grandfather always left for work every single morning around 4am and worked until 6pm that night. He had a two hour drive to work and was due on Fort Knox by 6am. He worked as a civilian mechanic for the U.S. military.

My aunt was the only one at home during these times, and she's always been a night owl. She stays up all night and then sleeps during the day. To me, playing hooky was the perfect crime.

Most of my attempts at hooky were botched because my grandmother knew me all too well to say the least.

Me playing hooky was to be expected. I was known for being a problematic child, and especially when it came to school attendance.

Now, having tasted the freedom of nearly a year without having to go to school, I was ready to move on to bigger better things. I wanted to stay home all day, chew tobacco, and play video games. Who wanted a high school diploma? I didn't.

My grandmother's solution to the problem was to stand outside every morning, or watch me from the window to ensure that I got on the bus.

This pretty much kept me from hooky altogether, as I deemed it more trouble than it was worth. Plus, hooky meant I couldn't be in the house all day, as I would get caught.

Second, I had absolutely nothing to do, and as I said I did not carry a cell phone at the time. I had no entertainment, and was better off just going to school. Even more so with the cold winter months approaching.

I would just go to school.

Skipping class was the answer to the problem. I didn't have to attend class anymore, I was still at school as far as my family knew, and while still bored to absolute shit, I was out of the cold for the day.

How I played hooky was to get off the bus,
go into school without other kids of my
grade noticing I was there and slipping off to
the bathroom. Where I would remain for the
entirety of the day. Just sitting on the toilet,
in a stall.
Sometimes I would just sit there reading
books. Other times I would practically piss
my pants when a teacher or principal would
come into the bathroom and take a really
long time.
My school year went on like this for the rest
of the year. I don't know if my parents knew
I played hooky within the school. It wasn't
known to me.
If I showed up to my first class, I would
become accounted for and the school
wouldn't call home. This was usually what I
would do, as my classes were stretched out,
a majority of the kids in my first class could
care less if I existed, and more than half
didn't even see me for the rest of the day. It
was the best option.

I played hooky at school for weeks.
Sometimes I attended classes, but I was
always sure to skip gym class. This worked
perfectly for the first month I did it.
Pretty soon somebody saw me show up one
day, and I had to go to gym class. The
school principal came into the restroom, and
had been waiting in there with me for nearly

15 minutes. When he realized I wasn't using the restroom, he told me to "Finish it up and get to class."

I about shit myself right there on the toilet. I knew I'd been caught and so for the rest of the day had to attend classes. After nearly a month of in-school hooky, I decided I had grown completely tired of this 'cat and mouse' game with the school authorities and just decided to go to class. It wasn't as boring, didn't smell like shit, and I still got to go to lunch. Anything beat sitting around chewing tobacco in a stall on an empty stomach.

That's really all it boiled down to, I hated not being able to chew my tobacco when I wanted.

A couple days of attending class began to bore me, and I'd try to find other ways to fill my time. I'd go to the library and rent books. I'd sit in the bathroom right before first class and read the bible for "strength" and I would urinate multiple times due to nervousness. I was losing the battle against my social anxiety.

My grandmother let down her guard one morning while I was at the bus stop trying to prepare myself for another day of this routine nonsense. "Just try to get through the day." I remember whispering to myself.

I looked back and noticed the blinds in the window overlooking my grandma's living room were not open. I knew she wasn't watching.

It was dark enough in the morning by this time as it was already late October. I knew I could use the dark to slip across the road in over the neighbor's fence to the large woodlands nearly a half a mile away. I could spend the day on an adventure, versus getting on the bus and dealing with being forced to soak and regurgitate useless information all day in the name of "education". Why not teach me how to write a check or file taxes? Why the hell did it even matter who founded America? We all know it was Leif Erikson, not Columbus.

I hesitated in the cold morning dew. The black sky overhead. I could see a thread of the rising sun on the horizon. I looked up at the stars.

Now or never. I looked around to be sure the bus wasn't coming. I looked back at my grandmother's window. Blinds still closed at this point. Just then I heard the bus coming up over the hill at the end of the road. That distinct diesel engine sound.

I quickly decided I wasn't going to school and darted across the road before the bus driver could clear the hill to spot me. I delved into the drop off on the side of the road opposite the driveway and laid in the overgrown waist high grass.

The bus approached my stop, and slowed down to a stop. I was hoping my grandma wasn't looking, and I don't think she was. The bus made the distinct noise of the air brake engaging. This would fool my grandma into thinking she heard the bus stop, and so would assume I must be getting on.

After a few seconds of me laying and hoping no kids on the bus had seen me laying in the grass, the bus took off. I had done it. I had successfully evaded detection, and fooled my grandma into thinking I was at school.

It was gonna be a day of adventure. I had my tobacco, and I had an idea. Today was gonna be great.

Or so I thought. Apparently diving into the wet grass wearing blue jeans, a t-shirt and a light jacket wasn't smart. As a result, I was soaking wet and it was like thirty-six degrees outside.

Now, my whole day was to endure the cold and still I had to trek far away from a warm house that I can't go into, and wait until time to come home.

The problem here being that I hadn't really thought all this through. I didn't have a lighter, and so I couldn't start a fire. Going back to the woods in this dark and cold morning would be a bad idea. This wasn't

going to be a successful hooky day. I didn't even have a watch to tell what time it was. Better to just go into the house and tell them I was playing hooky. If they tried to make me go, I wouldn't. Grandma had to be at work by eight that morning anyway, so If I waited until she went out to her truck to leave and then showed myself: she'd be pissed, but I would be in the clear.
That's precisely what happened that morning. She got mad, bitched a little and then drove to work. I was free to do what I wanted for the day. As most teenage boys did, I went in and fired up the old PC, put a chew of tobacco in and played "Age of Empires" for the rest of the day.

Another hooky attempt I played worked out successfully; they weren't always failures. I had pre packed a backpack full of survival gear, as I had no intention of going to school that day. It looked like my normal backpack, but instead had a kitchen knife, some string, a tarp, a lighter, some food, and a couple books, along with water and spare tobacco. Today, I was gonna play hooky come hell or high water.
That's precisely what I did. By now, my grandmother quit caring if I went to school or not, as she could not make me go. I went out this particular morning to the bus stop, like I always did.

Just as soon as grandma closed the blinds, I slipped across the road and over the fence. I disappeared into the black of the early November morning. I trekked well over a half a mile back into the woods where I decided to set up camp by the nearby spring. I strung a line of string between two trees, and laid out my tarp. I thought for sure today it was going to rain very soon, didn't want to be wet and cold. I then turned my attention towards making a fire.

Sticks, leaves, I gathered everything I could burn and attempted to start a fire. This was failed due to everything I was trying to light was completely wet. It had rained the night before, and the morning frost made this an impossible task with my limited knowledge at the time. I lay there, watching the sun come up, shivering in the morning cold, and thinking about walking all the way back to my grandma's.
It seemed like an entire hour passed. I still lay underneath the tarp, nothing to do but listen to the crows overhead.
Then I heard it. It was very faint, very distant, but I heard it. My grandmother was screaming my middle name. I knew when she screamed my middle name that I was going to be in trouble.

"Damn it to hell!" I yelled and crawled out

from underneath the tarp. The cold in my hands made them ache, and now here I was, all the way back in the woods, and had been caught. I thought she would've been at work by then, but turns out she didn't work that morning but rather later that afternoon. She was enjoying her morning cigarette when she got the phone call from the school that I was not there. Goddamnit, I knew I wasted all this time. She knew I was somewhere nearby. Where else could a kid without a car go?

I didn't go back home that day though; I wandered the woods after the clouds broke. It was surprisingly warm that day, and so I felt I might as well have an adventure. Around 9 or 10 that morning, I heard coyotes farther ahead in the woods nearly a mile away or more. I always wanted to see a coyote, so I went hiking deeper into the woods. Even though I never found a coyote that day, I still was doing something with my time. I was bored to shit, and didn't want to go home and get yelled at, so I just walked around.

At some point I had decided to go up on the hill across from my grandmother's house and lay underneath a tree. I knew she wouldn't see me, and yet I would be able to wait for the afternoon bus to appear. The plan at this point was to wait for the bus to stop, and then I'd say that I had been at school the whole time. That there must've been some paperwork mistake because I was at school. I just didn't answer the teacher when she looked for me in class this morning, yeah, that's it.

My grandma appeared after several hours, out in her driveway approaching her truck. I had been underneath the old cedar tree this whole time, reading books and chewing tobacco.

When I saw this, I immediately sat up because my plans had changed. If my aunt was asleep, then I could slip into the house and get warm, as it was still somewhat chilly outside, not due to the sun but because of how breezy the midwest is.

My grandma got into her truck, and I made out that she was in her work uniform. She drove off moments later, and that's when I said to hell with waiting anymore. I made my way off the hill, over the fence and back into the yard. I was counting on my aunt being asleep.

When I opened the front door to the house, I heard my aunt in the kitchen. She began scowling at me saying that "Mom was pissed off." and that I was a damn punk. Really just boiled down to her not wanting me home at the time. As I said, she really does not like her sister's kids as she feels we robbed her of her life. Technically she

did that, by not learning to drive, dropping out of school and abusing cold medicine and prescription pills all the time.
I won't throw stones at her though. I do give her credit for taking care of us. She tried to do what she could. She was the same age I was at the time of having to raise my brother and I: only sixteen.
I spent the rest of the day on the computer, like always. I'd face my punishment later, always did.
Like I said though, my grandmother didn't ever hit us children, and so coming from a violent background where that was the only way to show us we were wrong, I didn't think I did anything wrong; or at least in my eyes had nothing to worry about.

Then came the day I was called into the principal's office. He sat me down and wanted to have a long chat as to why out of half of the school year, I had missed half that much. I had no answer for it. He basically told me that he would like me to go home and tell my mother that signing me out of school would be the best option. He insisted that he did not like recommending this option, but that he didn't feel I was cut out for school. I told him I'd rather come to school. Really at that point I don't know what I was thinking.
A couple months go by, it's February near

the week before Valentine's Day.

I had mentioned to my mother sometime during that week that the principal wanted me signed out of school. She immediately agreed, and said she would take me to do it that Thursday or Friday, can't recall the day to be honest.

When the day came, I was never happier. I was ready to walk through those doors one final time and sign those papers. I looked at what few friends I made, and not once told them what was going on. I just marched straight to the principal's office, hellbent on freedom.

My mother talked to the principal, and he apologized for the recommendation, but he felt that I would be held back another year, and would repeat ninth grade again. That it would be better off if I was signed out of school and enrolled in a GED program. My mom apologized on my behalf and signed the papers without hesitation.

When I left that school with my mother by my side, I remember her telling me that I was free. I was ecstatic, I mean, what kid wouldn't be? I was going to taste all the freedom I had the year prior back in 2009. I popped in a big pinch of tobacco in my lip, turned on "Freebird" and watched as we pulled slowly away from the school parking lot. I'll never forget feeling so rid of all the anxiety that came from that high school. At least since having discovered the beauty of computers, the few months of computer class I did taught me how to type. It was a skill I'd always wanted, and school helped me get that at least.

Time to go home, and be free.

13. "Man's best friend"

I grew up around dogs. From the moment I could walk to this very day, I've known a dog or two. Today however, I'm a cat person all the way. I don't really like dogs as much as I used to, and I have a very good reason for that. The reason being is that I just have too many bad memories.

Rather than just telling you I'm a cat person, I'd like to tell you why.

It all started back when I had been a preteen. I really loved a poodle that I nicked named "Poo-Poo" as the dog had a tendency to eat shit all the time. Actual shit, and he didn't care the source. He'd eat it off the ground, cat shit, dog shit, rabbit pellets. All of it.

Despite it all, I loved this dog. He was a wild little thing, always running around. He followed us kids to the bus stop every morning and then would walk back home. This was an impressive feat to me because this bus stop was à 5 minute walk down a dead end street to our house. There were several houses down this street, but ours was the only gravel driveway that lead up a steep hill to our trailer.

Now the bus couldn't come down our street to get us, and so that's why we had to walk every single morning to the bus stop, come rain or snow.

Now then, this dog would follow us down this long street every morning, see us on the bus, and then walk home. It was routine every single day.

Poo-poo was my best friend at the time, my

stepdad would make fun of me for being fat, isolated me from the rest of the family for being a "(Mylastname)-bitch" and would make me eat away from the table, from "his kids." I especially hated when he would kick my dog for no good reason.
It became that I would always find joy in this dog, during these hard times. When I would go to the local store, Poo-poo would follow me against my will. I would try to make him stay home, but he just would not listen to me. This was problematic because I cared a great deal about my dog's safety and I did not want him to get into the road: potentially getting ran over or maimed by a vehicle. My solution to this, was I would put him in my shirt, as he was a toy poodle: so he fit quite nicely.
I would tuck my shirt in at the bottom, so that Poo-poo would be safe, and not fall out. I would then slowly ride my bike on the sidewalk to the store. My dog was my best friend, and I wanted the best for him: so while at the store I would buy him his favorite treat. Not as a reward for him following me, but because I felt sorry for how my stepdad treated this poor dog. Poo-poo loved liver cheese, for whatever reason.
He did the happiest little dances for liver cheese. That dog was like a ball of fluffy lightning, all over the place. He'd eat it and always want more. Like an empty pit or something, he'd eat the whole container if he could.
One morning, my brothers and I walked to the bus stop to go to school, per usual Poo-poo followed. By now, I would always make sure he was in the

house, but my baby sister wanted to tell me goodbye that morning and let the dog back out after I was already down the hill. Turning back would ensure I'd miss the bus at this point, and would result in me getting beat; I didn't want to risk it. Poo-poo had gone home on his own so many times before, that I hoped he would go home today like he always did.

The bus rolls up after a few minutes, I'm finishing my cigarette and worrying over my dog, telling him I loved him and wanted him to go back home like a good boy that he was. The bus driver opens the doors and my brothers and I get on the bus. The bus driver takes off and I can see the expression in her face change instantly. I look out at the bus stop as the bus pulls off and I don't see my dog. I panic. I want to cry. Where was my Poo-poo?
The bus had to circle around to drive by my stop again, as it didn't stop at that particular location again. I saw my dog in the road. Obviously dead. I hid my tears, and tried to not show emotion. One of the kids made a comment that there's "red mashed potatoes in the road" and laughed. It wasn't funny, the pain in my chest was unbearable.

A kind neighbor lady saw what had happened, she went and got our dog and put him in a shoe box with a towel wrapped around him. I remember opening the box and crying so hard.
My mother telling me that it was "my fault" and if I hadn't let him out this morning it wouldn't have

happened. I hadn't let him out this morning, my baby sister did. Had my mother not been on her dead ass asleep in the bed, she could have prevented my dog from getting hit.

Rather, her routine was to let our stepdad get us up in the morning, with violent yells, verbal slander, and "get our dumb fucking asses to the bus stop." Had she been watching my three year old sister at the time, she would never have opened the door. It wasn't my fault. Why would you place that blame on a young boy who just turned thirteen? That was fucked up.

I'll never forget burying Poo-poo. I was told to go dig a hole for him and bury him and that's what I did. My step dad said I should just throw him over the fence into the woods and be done with it.

I dug the hole, and covered my best friend up with a towel; I didn't want him to get dirt on his face. I proceeded to cover him with dirt, crying all the way. I must have cried a tear for every scoop of dirt. Heart broken. I said a little prayer for my puppy in hopes that the Lord would hear it. Praying that I one day be free of this nightmare, praying that my puppy was safe in heaven. I found comfort in the fact that my stepdad couldn't kick Poo-poo anymore. At least Poo-poo didn't have to suffer like I did. He was free.

The Lord giveth, and the Lord taketh away.

A few months later, we get a golden retriever named Hunter. Hunter was a very energetic dog of medium build. He was good with kids, and was initially obtained to be my little sister's dog. Well, he loved everybody. A better dog for a kid, you probably couldn't have found one. We get home from school one day after having Hunter for several months, to find him dead by the trailer with a single rifle shot just behind his left armpit.

Apparently he had been running around the neighbor's yard across the trailer park and somebody decided to shoot. Why not call the cops on someone shooting within city limits, you might ask? I don't know. The trailer park was in a large field and was surrounded by woodland. Nobody called the cops in that town, as it was a shitty little rural town full of trouble and drugs. I guess that explains it then.

Hunter was dead, I felt sad for him but had not yet got over losing my Poo-poo just months before, so I hadn't really gotten attached to him.

I didn't like the fact that such a good dog would be shot for no fucking reason, but there he lay. No justice for this poor innocent animal. Damn trailer trash across the fence, that wasn't the only time they had done something like this.

We once had another dog from a litter of puppies that I loved very much. She went by the name Heavy. We raised her and she was a very loyal dog, always happy to see us. She'd love to play fetch and run all over the hillside looking for tennis balls. She'd go grab it, come back and have me throw it over and over and over. There was no end to the times she would have you do this.

We happened to have another litter of puppys from a stray that had been living with us at the time, and these puppies were old enough by now to be running around outside on their own.

I come back from the store one day, and see Heavy eating something. I mean, she's really chewing this stuff up like it's candy or something. I grow curious instantly, because why would it have the texture of dog food but not stand out from the grass? The puppies were eating it right alongside of her.

That's when to my horror as I approach I see a bag of rat poison. Panic set in. I took the poison immediately and put it where the dogs couldn't get it and grabbed what I could off of the ground.

I grabbed the puppies and Heavy and ran inside to tell my mother what had happened. She calls our stepdad who says to not take them to the vet as he said we didn't have the money, but give them hydrogen peroxide.

That was the thing, we didn't have any. He rushes home with some peroxide he bought at the Dollar store, pissed off and upset that his dogs were poisoned. He makes my little brother hold the dog's mouths open as he dumps peroxide down their throats.

I'm trying to comfort the puppies, meanwhile. Some of them began to convulse, one was bleeding out its nose; it was a miserable and sickening sight. Heavy vomited up green foam, and chunks of rat poison, as did most of the puppies. The one who bled out the nose ended up dying that very night.

We were unable to save her.
These animals didn't deserve that. If I hadn't acted
when I did I don't think any of them would have
made it. Time was of the essence in this situation.
Looking back, even if my parents had taken them to
the vet at that time of night, none of the animals
would have survived. The distance from our trailer
to the local veterinary clinic would have taken
nearly an hour to get to.

We looked at the rat poison bag, to determine its
origin. We didn't know of any store in our area to
carry that type of poison. We determined that the
poison must've came from the other part of the
trailer park as for one: Heavy was over there earlier
that day as she played with the children over there
and two: these people have killed our dogs before,
for absolutely no reason.
Heavy was known to chase their chickens, which
gave them a reason to try and get rid of her. We
assumed somebody gave her the bag of poison,
and being the dog she was, she hauled it home to
share with the puppies she'd grown fond of.
This stuff was fish flavored, so no doubt that this
was done to target our pets.

A couple years later, I had long since moved out to
my grandmother's house. Heavy was around five
years old at the time.
She apparently had suffered from heart damage
from being subject to rat poison from the years
prior, as she suddenly collapsed dead without

cause. My family said she was barking a lot and then foaming at the mouth, dead on the ground. She was buried by my stepdad, who was distraught his dog had passed away. I did love Heavy, and if this was supposed to be karma, I didn't like it because Heavy didn't deserve to die like that. The trash across the fence was to blame for all of this.

At the summer of 2011, I was sixteen soon to be turning seventeen that autumn.
I had returned to my mother's house for the final time in my youth. We adopted a puppy named Sarge. I thought my stepdad's naming skills were garbage, and that he always tried to name his dogs "badass" names to try and look tough. Yeah, good luck intimidating any grown man you weak little woman beating coward.
I digress, Sargento was what I called the puppy. I didn't like that my stepfather always tried to make the dogs he had mean. I was raised to treat dogs like your own children by my grandmother, and so I did the same with Sargento.
My stepfather would try and beat the pup, would smack it in the face for urinating on the floor, and would then rub its nose in it before in a series of the puppy's yelps, toss the pup out the front door into the night.
This happened on numerous occasions. My stepdad would get mad at for me for playing with the puppy and babying it, as it was gonna make it "soft". I still played with the puppy anyway, because at that point, the fucking prick I called a stepdad

didn't scare me anymore. Fuck him and what he said, that puppy was my little buddy.

I'd buy Sargento treats, we'd play with toys, and he'd chase me outside in the yard. He was such a good boy. I'd rub his little tummy while he slept and kiss his little nose, only to be surprised with him licking me back.

One day, my mother attacked me for not doing her laundry right. In actuality, I had done her laundry in her own separate load. My youngest brother at the time, who was a spawn of my stepdad, put his clothes in on top of my mother's clothes because he didn't want to wash his own clothes. Well, I was to answer for this.

My mother began cussing me, the usual "retard" type name calling. Whatever at this point, right? Heard it for nearly ten years every single day.

I stand up to her, she threatens to put my head in the fridge. "Go right ahead and try." I said.

I'll be damned if I hadn't gotten the sentence out that the 6'0 tall, 400 lbs giant that is my mother, leapt up and proceeded to grab me by the throat and slam my head in the refrigerator. I was skilled at fighting at this point; growing up like I did and having fist fought my step dad. That later ended him ever touching me physically again, because I laid him out one morning and shattered his dentures; which to this day haven't been fixed. He says they hurt his mouth but I let that be a reminder to the piece of trash.

Anyways, I would never hit my mama in a million
years. I didn't this morning either as my head
bounced off the refrigerator repeatedly. Rather, I
used my smaller frame to rotate and face her and
then shoved her off me. She swung at me and I
shoved her again. I was crying, begging her to stop.
I realized I'd bitten off more than I could chew. I
ended up with a busted lip and a little sore, but
otherwise I stopped her assault. I retreated out of
the house immediately after to the storage shed
where I lived.

I ran away that day and ended up being gone for
two days. All the while little Sargento was coming
down with Parvo and I didn't even know it.

I hitchhiked that day nearly twenty miles and landed
into a small town around dusk, where all I had on
me was a light jacket and a small knife. I hadn't
even brought food with me.

I spent the night in some person's barn without
permission, and arose the next day before sunrise
to decide what to do next.

A blister on my foot caused me to take my shoe off
and I carried my shoe in my arm. It was a Sunday
afternoon and so one of the churches I passed by a
few people took notice of me. Instead of offering
help, they called the state police.

I guess they thought I was on drugs or drunk, I
don't know. I was a sixteen year old boy who was
limping with a massive blister on the side of my foot
from not wearing socks. The state trooper gave me
a ride home in the back of his cruiser; he said he
wasn't going to leave a minor on the side of a

highway.

By the time I returned home, Sargento was not acting right. He isn't eating or drinking. I told my mom but she basically neglected the issue as it wasn't important to her at the time. I try to get Sargento to eat, but all he did was lay out on the porch. I brought him into the storage building with me that night, with a bowl of water and some food. I laid him on my chest petting him and telling him it was gonna be alright.
I fell asleep with him on my chest. At some point during the night, I dreamed of Sargento. He wasn't speaking but I knew he was telling me goodbye.
I awoke that morning to find Sargento had crawled off of my chest, made his way to the opposite wall, and died on my blanket in the corner. As I said, this was summer, I lived in a metal storage building and not in the trailer at this point. I had no air conditioning; I had one single box fan.
There was no need for the blanket to be on me. Little Sargento died facing me, and that hurt me so much. That pain in my chest returned. Another best friend.
It's like you feel so much pain but it won't come out. You don't quite know how to handle the situation; almost like it's too much to process.
When I ran into the trailer that morning crying, my mother told me she "didn't want to hear my retarded ass" and that I needed to "get the fuck out of her house with that bullshit" and not to come back inside until I had something else to talk about.

I was devastated.

What kind of life was this? Why let a little dog die just to hurt my feelings? What bothers me the most to this day is that I never thought of asking for help. Who could've helped me? How?

I buried little Sargento in a shallow grave. I didn't even pray this time. There was no god. Any god that would give someone a life like this: just to suffer, and take all his best friends away- was a maniac. A sadomasochistic tyrant. There was no hope. Nothing.

God was gone. My friend was gone. I had nobody.

Rest in peace, Sargento.

14. "The Sound of Madness"

This is the turn of my story. This final time I
returned to my mother's from my grandmother's
would be the hardest time in my life I ever faced. It
would be the peak of my mother's abuse, and the
justice for all the years I was abused by my
stepdad. I was soon to be seventeen when I
returned to my mother's house in July of 2010.
My birthday was that fall, as I mentioned before. I
endured the usual name calling by my mother, but
this would be the worst yet. When I finally left my
mother's house this time, the emotional and
psychological abuse took its toll. I ended up having
panic attacks repeatedly. To think about the things
that happened to me there, makes me cry to this
day. I was traumatised by what they did to me.
My mother always cracked jokes and laugh as she
called me "the child called IT" but I don't think she'd
realize that one day I would obtain my GED and
become an author, only to make public the trauma
she did to me. The damage is done, nothing can
take away the pain of being isolated and abused
like that. Nobody deserves that.
Without further adieu, hear is the part of my life that
changed me forever.

The year of 2010: the year I dropped out at the age
of sixteen during that February. I spent all this time
at my grandma's and then returned to my mother's
house willingly towards the end of July that year. I
had returned for a very stupid reason; that reason

was my brother was always coming out to my grandmother's house.

It would've been okay, but he was always being a jackass and pushing my buttons. That, or he was always trying to intimidate me. My brother by now, the one I called "Bub" earlier in this story; had grown to 6'3 and weighed 350 lbs. I was still 5'11 but had gained a lot of body fat from my poor diet at my grandmas.

Still, my brother was bigger than me. I didn't want to hurt my brother. I didn't want to fight anymore, I had saw there was no need to fight anyone. Violence wasn't the answer and I was starting to see that by now.

He was a bully, and although he didn't bully me, he would try to provoke me to violence. I ended up just leaving, and returned to my mom's. I thought that I didn't have anything to worry about. This would be a walk in the park like it had been before.

I admittedly had been abusing gasoline at this point in my life. I hated myself. I didn't want to be alive anymore, I was a worthless loser who would never have an education. I escaped through huffing gasoline. I would "huff" the fumes by breathing them in. Sometimes I would dump a little gasoline on a rag and sniff the fumes, sometimes I would put my mouth above the opening of a gas can and suck the fumes into my lungs. I didn't care about anyone or anything. I didn't care about my future. I spent a large majority of 2010 high on gasoline. The effects being I would hallucinate, have heightened senses,

and have a slight dizzy effect from it.
I saw things that were not there. Perhaps the
reason I did it was because it ripped me from the
reality of being 'His' son. I thought myself better off
dead.
My grandparents knew I had been abusing gasoline
and my grandfather began locking the gas cans up.
This didn't stop me, as I went and huffed gasoline
out of the riding mower. It was cheap and got me
high, and had the plus side of killing me. I was in a
very dark place in my life at that point, and the
impulsivity that comes with being a juvenile
teenager doesn't exactly help the situation. I was so
reckless that I would huff gasoline while smoking
cigarettes.
I would draw in the fumes from the gas, and then
take a drag off of my lit cigarette. I'm lucky to have
survived this ordeal, needless to say.
My grandmother was scared she was going to find
me dead in the yard one day and they begged me
to quit huffing gas. I just never listened. I would huff
until I'd black out. I wouldn't remember anything or
having blacked out: whole minutes and hours of my
life was seemingly missing. I would just pass out for
five to ten minutes and then snap back awake.

This was further made dangerous not only by
smoking by an open container of gasoline with
flammable fumes still in my lungs, but exacerbated
further by passing out in very frigid temperatures,
wearing nothing more than a light jacket and jeans.
Once, I blacked out in nothing but a shirt and jeans.

I came to with frostbitten hands. My life had no value at that point and time.

Today, it's that time in my life that I regret the most, because I ended up with slight brain damage. I have memory problems, and cannot speak without stuttering on my words. It was a very dear price for a very valuable lesson.

My brother came out one day to my grandmother's, and I went back to my mother's house. There during July to September it wasn't all that bad. I fell in love with my puppy Sargento, and while you already now know the story, this was before the first physical attack by my mother that September morning over laundry.

Life was okay. My mother wasn't always a monster, she had her good traits. She took us out for pizza, bought us stuff, gave us money and bought us tobacco. She loved us in her own fucked up way, I think.

After mom attacked me that morning, she proceeded to make my life a living nightmare. I wasn't allowed to eat at the table anymore, but this time not because I wasn't one of my stepdad's chosen kids, but because she called me "faggot". To her, in her very own chosen words she referred to me as "A goddamned queer." and I was treated horribly because of this. Now, the story to how I got this name stems from the fact that my mother had a couple sex toys- artificial penises. These, along with the gay porn she had in her room went missing. I did not touch them, but I did know the sibling that did. I knew my brother was gay, he told me that. I didn't care that he was, I loved him all the same. Him being gay didn't make me think any less of him, but I knew what would happen if my parents found out.

I never snitched on him about the dildo covered in shit I found in his closet, or the gay porn I found in the DVD player. I had my honor code to my family, even if it was my family attacking me.
My mom kept saying I took it, that I was responsible. When I would deny it but not say I knew where it was, she'd slap me and tell me to get the fuck out of her house.
So, every night I ate on the counter come supper time, standing and facing away from my family while my mother called me a "faggot" from across the room. I could feel her boring holes through the back of my head with her eyes.
I tried to ignore her, but this time everything seemed to be getting to me personally.
I told her once that I had become an atheist, and she told me to "Get that satanic shit out of her house."
Had she found out my poor brother was a homosexual, I can only imagine his punishment. I kept my mouth shut. Regardless of what he did, he was my brother. I wouldn't let her do to him what she did to me.
This, alongside being hit everyday, I became submissive to my mother's wishes. I did exactly what she wished, when she wished me to do it

without question. I couldn't always avoid her verbal abuse or slaps to my face, but I tried my best. If she was having an off day, she would target me. I pissed her off once that winter, and she threw me out into the cold in nothing more than a shirt and jeans. I curled up in the fetal position on the front porch, trying to avoid laying in the snow and ice. I was lucky that the dryer was running. The heat from the dryer vent allowed me to endure the cold for that entire hour I was outside. I lay with my shirt pulled over my knees, my arms held close to my body to preserve what heat I had left. This situation was nothing new to me. I had been thrown in the snow many times before. Sometimes if the dryer wasn't on, I would go and exercise to keep warm. It wasn't always effective but it did help me stay somewhat warm enough.

Once I found a wet sleeping bag outside that was frozen to the ground. I crawled down inside of it and while I ended up soaking wet and still cold, there was a small amount of warmth. Anything was better than standing there waiting to die. I couldn't give up. That's what she wanted me to do. I was not a quitter. I was a fighter, and it's this mentality that allowed me to see those horrible times through.

By the time my mother let me back inside, she would think I had learned my lesson by standing up for myself. I had been quite uncomfortable out in the cold, but I would stand up for myself again without question. There was no lesson to be learned, I wasn't calling her names. I wasn't doing anything but objecting to the accusation. This would send her into a frenzy and would result in me being hit with something or the object of flurries of open handed slaps to the face. Sometimes she'd wait to catch me off guard, grab me by the shirt and punch me in the face. That happened sometimes too, and I hated surprise attacks. I was always watching out for my mother to attack me. Always on the alert for indication of an attack of future assault. Always.

Mom hated me. I remember going to the hospital with her and she told me that she hated my guts. That I was "Not her real kid." that she "Didn't give a fuck about me." and that "I was worthless, nothing to her." as she put it. That her 'real' children were the ones my stepdad had with her.
Those words cut me like a knife; I never forgot those words. Tears pooled in my eyes in that hospital room, and I fell silent. Not even to this day have I forgotten how she made me feel; but I'll tell you one thing. I lost my love for her that day; no, not all at once. It died slowly from that point forward. I waited on her hand and foot, day and night. I fixed dinner. I washed all of the laundry. I cleaned every single day. I mopped the floors. I even got out of my bed at 2 am to cook her grilled cheese sandwiches, simply because she wanted them. I helped the other children with their school work. I got them ready for school every morning. I had been changing diapers since I was twelve years old. I had to burp and feed my infant siblings since I was eleven.
This was how my mama repaid me for all the good I

had done. She blamed me for "fucking her life up" and that I ruined her life by being born. Why didn't I blame her for taking my childhood from me? Why not give her a taste of her own medicine? That's not the person I am. I'm a grown man now. I'll be halfway to sixty in just four more years. I'm married, with my own house today. This childhood is all behind me.

Back then, I did blame my mother for all the things she did to me.

I forgave my mother, not because of her. I forgave her for me.

I forgave her because hatred is too great a burden to bear. For the simple fact that I don't live in the past anymore. She took my life, but that's fine. Karma has returned the favor to her, and I'll explain more on that later.

That winter, my mother ended up in the hospital. She had a blood clot in her lung, and this resulted in her staying in the hospital for over two entire months.

Dead of winter, my stepdad took off work to be with my mother in the hospital. He left me and my second oldest brother home alone for a majority of these two months. The other siblings he came and picked up at the end of every school week. Never leaving Bub and I any money or food.

Neither of us can drive at this point, despite me being seventeen and of legal driving age. We live in a trailer on a hill and the closest store is a mile away. We have no money.

The worst part of this story is remember that I weighed over 200 lbs at my grandmas just that summer? Turns out going to bed hungry without food those two months dropped me down to 160 lbs. My brother and I lived off of scraps we threw together. Stale bread, mayonnaise and imitation bacon bits were a staple as we would make sandwiches out of them. After eating only one meal a day, our food supply began to diminish at the end of week two. I had to feed these children every single day during the school week, plus my brother and I.

At the end of every week, just like I said, our stepdad would take "his kids" to the hospital, where they would get to eat Papa John's pizza, Chinese takeout, and McDonald's.

Bub and I continued to starve back at the trailer. I said fuck it, after seeing a jug of spare change in my stepdad's van.

I unlocked the door and stole it. I was hungry, I had all these mouths to feed; I would take an ass beating if I had to, but we needed food.

We could go no longer without food at this point. I had long since ran out of tobacco and so wasn't even addicted anymore at this point.

I remember the first thing I did was walk all the way to the store with my brother, and we bought some hamburger meat, lettuce, cheese, lunch meat and bread along with a couple cases of sodas. We went home and I made us all some food. We ate like kings that night.

Days went on like that, sometimes we ate.

Sometimes we went to bed hungry. All I know is that "his kids" didn't starve at all.

Once that the other kids complained we were out of food at home, then my step dad went and bought groceries on a Friday he happened to be down at the trailer.
This was my life. I was the man of the house from December of 2010 to February of 2011.
My brother and I roamed around the woods and found our bond as brothers finally strengthening after all this time. We made the best of the hellish living conditions and most importantly survived.
The highlight of all this, is that Bub and I would go out into the woods near our trailer, and hang out at this old barn. We would make pine needle tea and talk about life. I would tell him about the woods, various survival skills and how to live off the land. We would prank call people on his cell phone. We were brothers.

15. "Setting Forth"

My mother return home February of that year. That's when the real trouble began. While she was in the hospital she also gave birth to my littlest brother. During the whole events between July to February she was pregnant during 2010. I remember the day we went and picked him up from the hospital up in Louisville. I was happy to see him, but I knew what it was going to be.

As usual it would be me raising another child, while she slept all the time, and I was right.

That's exactly what it ended up happening. The last years of my teenage life was spent taking care of an infant. I spent most of my life taking care of kids so this wasn't anything new to me. It's like I'd end up changing diapers. I've probably changed so many in my life that I can't even count them all. I never had a childhood.

Except for the few years that I spent in my grandmother's, I never got the truly see what it was like to be a little kid. My mother used my whole life to be a slave for her, to do the things that she didn't want to do around the house. And to raise kids that she didn't want to raise. She was okay with getting me hooked on tobacco, she wanted me to die young. She wanted me to not have a life. She didn't want to see me go to school, she didn't want to see me live my dreams, and she made this all very clear to me.

Especially during the year of 2010. It was during

this time that I had lost all respect for my mother and slowly, gradually I lost all of my love I would potentially had for her.

It came no surprise later after 2 months of dealing with the same squalling infant, I would get up out of the bed at at 2 in the morning to her screaming at me to take care of that "little bastard" as she referred to him.

This lasted two months of my life before I finally decided that I had had enough and that I wasn't going to be her little slave anymore. I was going to stand up to the bully that was my mother.

That's exactly what I did. My grandmother had come over to get me (think it was around in April). She was going to take me birthday shopping, because I hadn't got to go that year prior. My mother was not happy at this and she told me to have my ass back there about 12 at night. Now my grandmother had a strong habit of staying out late at stores. And, what I mean by this, is the woman would go at like 7 p.m. at night and she would not return until like 7 or 8 the next morning. It was during this time that she shopped.

I remember talking to my grandmother that night at Denny's as we sat eating food. I was asking if I could come back home. I told her that I was sorry for how I had behaved back when I was 16. I apologize dearly for everything that I had done. I told her that I would not make that mistake again. She told me that my aunt didn't want me back there, and so that's the way it was going to be.

We ended up going to Walmart later that night. I
think if I remember right I moved around the store
thinking that my grandma really didn't give a fuck
about me either; or at least that's how she made
me feel. I understand and I was wrong in some of
the things that I did at my grandmother's house. I
realized that it was my fault for all the stupid things
that I did. But I was just a dumb 16 year old boy. I
thought I was a man, I thought I knew it all; I
thought I was on top of the world. I wasn't shit. My
mother didn't give a damn about me and I told her
my mom had told me all these things.

She told me that I should just go ahead and look
past it because my mother is mentally ill. It's always
the excuse my mom's mentally ill. She doesn't have
to face consequences to her actions because she's
mentally ill. That's how it goes. Now, remember my
mom told me to have my ass back there about 12
that night?
She wanted me home by midnight. I told my
grandmother this but my grandmother didn't really
care. She had shopping to do.
Upon going home the next morning, I arrived there
sometime at 7 a.m.

I tried to sneak into the house quietly but my
mother was already awake. She called me a
"Stupid mother fucker" as she sat there rocking the
baby.
The same baby that she had used to rob me of my

life. Her excuse for how she treated me after all this was over, was that it was because she was pregnant and her hormones were acting up.
All the physical abuse, all the verbal abuse, all the emotional trauma; all because she had hormones and they acted up on her.
I'm supposed to just walk on and forgive what she did at that point?
The things she did that made me have panic attacks and I broke down and cried years later while I was living in my grandmother's house.
These very things I was supposed just overlook because she had a hormone imbalance due to pregnancy? No.

This particular morning I decided finally I had had enough. I had toyed with the idea of going off and hitchhiking again as I had enjoyed my first experience back when I was still 16.

I had always kept the backpack ready to go in case of a situation like this, and I knew I was ready at this point, I had spent a whole winter sleeping out in a garden shed.
A metal building with no insulation, no heater, no nothing.
This was the life I was supposed to just lay down and take because of my father's actions? Because my mother had sex with him? And she claims I ruined her life, that it was my fault.

This morning in particular I wasn't having any more

of it. I told her if she couldn't treat me like a human being, that I wasn't going to be her son.

With that I packed my bags and took what I could carry on my back, I immediately began walking out to my grandmother's house. And the last words that my mother told me was that if I left that hill she was going to call the law.

I falsely threatened her with something I knew that she was getting away with illegally and promised her I would snitch if she said anything. This was the check mate that I needed to keep her off my ass. I walk out to my grandmother's house going to say goodbye one last time before I hit the old open road.

I ended up living there for the next three years of my life, but that's a different story.

Flashback 5 months prior, my step dad convinced his children that I was nothing more than their slave. As I was helping my little sister with her school work, she tossed her dishes in the sink still with food on the plate that I had just simply asked her to put in there since I had already washed all the dishes prior. The fact of her just tossing the dishes with food on them pissed me off as I taught them all to scrape their food on their plate into the trash; so, she knew I would have to get the dishes back out and scrap them for her.

I asked her "What did she think I was, her slave?" Her response was "Yes."

She thought the only reason that I was there was to take care of her and her siblings. And while she was only six at the time when she told me this, it hurt me deep because that was my little sister I cared so much for. She had been brainwashed to think that I was nothing more than a piece of trash forced there to take care of those kids.

I kept hearing rumors through my siblings that my step dad was saying that he was going to beat my ass; he was going to do this, he was going to do that. So I get up one particular morning, and by now I'd already been diagnosed with bipolar disorder and I hadn't had my medication.

That isn't an excuse for what was about to take place.
As I go through the front door, I hear my step dad in the back room talking shit about me saying that I was garbage and that I didn't do anything around the house and stuff.
So, as I walk to the back of the trailer where my family's all at, those kids had been saying that their daddy could whoop my ass. All of this was the build-up events that took place all in a short amount of time over a span of a few weeks.

At this point I was sick and tired of all his drama, and it was time he got beat like a man. The same way he beat me growing up. All the times he ripped off his shirt saying "Fight me!" to a 9 year old boy who was just trying to visit his mother from his grandma's house.
I walked back in that room and silence fell in the

house.
He knew he got caught talking shit. I tried to play
cool and talk to everybody and I told him what
those kids had told me; that I was nothing more
than a slave.
I said that hurt my feelings and I felt disrespected,
and I would like for somebody to explain to these
kids that I wasn't a slave. He wouldn't look at me,
but calmly said "I'll discipline my kids the way I see
fit."

These were the wrong words to say to me at this
point in time, which he soon realized.
Within seconds I had him up in a chokehold and
began to strangle the life out of him. The kids
began to cry, my mom began to panic, and I had
this little weasel up in my arms squeezing the life
right out of him. He was going to get what he finally
deserved. Knocking his teeth out at 13 wasn't good
enough for me. I lost my grip at some point and he
spun around to swing at me.
I caught his fist before he could even get a punch
off. I slammed him against the wall; had him by the
throat with another hand.
I put him in a headlock and began to pound his
face.
Meanwhile, my mother had already jumped up from
the bed, ran over to me, and began punching me in
the face and kicking me in the nuts. I felt none of
this taking place. Any pain that I felt was ignored
completely by my rage. I was beating him like the
way he beat me as a little child. He was getting his

just desserts for all the years that he abused me.
I unloaded on him like I should have done years
ago and he got every punch that he deserved. To
this day I do not regret it.

The first reaction that he had when I let him go was
running into the other room and calling the police.
The irony being is that I was the one that could
have called the police on him all those years that I
would get slapped from one end of the trailer to the
other.
He deserved his ass whooping. And now that he
got it he was trying to call for help.
I found out that this man that I feared as a little boy
was nothing more than a no-good coward. He was
not a man. A man doesn't go around beating on
children and trying to intimidate little boys to make
themselves feel better. They don't beat up on little
13 year old kids that are just trying to make him a
damn cup of coffee in the morning.
And a man, damn sure doesn't slap pregnant
women.
He's not a man. I never regretted anything about
showing him he was a weakling to me.
The state police showed up, threatened me with
taking me to jail. Didn't mean anything to me at this
point. I was like, "Go ahead and take me." My
mother made my stepdad drop the charges.
I was already in jail at that point, at least it would be
warmer where I was sleeping compared to sleeping
out in a little garden shed.

So, back to the story, I was at my grandmother's getting ready to leave and head off for the open road. My grandmother came outside and I explained what had happened. I told her what was going on and then spent the next three days doubled over with a stomach ache because I was so worried about going back to that hellhole. She assured me that I wouldn't have to and my mom was okay with me being out there too. My grandma realized what she had done was wrong, by not letting me come back to live with her. She agreed that it would be better off that I stayed with her. My grandmother went and bought me groceries to eat, but I didn't even eat anything for two days. I worried so much that I literally gave myself an ulcer, and I had to go to the hospital for medication.

This was the sad story of my life at this point, and I'm not writing this to try and get pity, I really don't want anybody's pity. It's clear it was a sorry existence for a 17 year old boy to have to deal with this kind of shit. Other kids my age was getting excited about going to college and finishing their high school years. And here I was worried about whether or not I was going to go back to the hell hole and be abused more.

I ended up not having to go back and so for that I was grateful. I slowly recovered from my ulcer I have developed, and beyond that everything is history. I think occasionally I ended up having to babysit but my mom paid me money and she didn't treat me nowhere near as bad as she was before.

On my 18th birthday, I went over to my mom's house to get my personal files that all 18 year olds should have such as social security card and birth certificate.

Oh, and all she told me was that I was a man now. That was that; not long after, they all moved up to the city and everything was fine by their means. However, I was left to clean up the emotional mess that I was after all the events I went through. Being back at my grandmother's after going through it all, the first thing that hurt me the most was the silence. I'd been in the situation where there was noise and chaos and I was constantly having to get up in the middle of the night and take care of a screaming baby. I had to cook supper and if I fucked it up I got beat. I wasn't allowed to eat at the table; I lived in a tiny little shed. I was always looking to be attacked again.

Now, in complete contrast to what I was used to, I was in a completely safe environment that didn't make any sense to me. I ended up going to counseling for the trauma that I suffered. I assure you now that it did not help me in the slightest.

16. "Moving on"

So after the story, after all was said and done and I became an adult, you might wonder how I ended up in life. Well, the first thing I tried to do was join the military, but because of my anxiety disorder I was unable to do so. Since I suffered from bipolar disorder as well, that pretty much kept me from joining the military on its own. I spent the next three years of my life living in my grandmother's up until I was 20 years old. Mainly because not having a childhood made me feel like enjoying the care-free life my grandma allowed me to live. I was also still dealing with the trauma to the point that I would have nightmares. Eventually though, I recovered.

Through my escape of using chewing tobacco, I developed my first cancerous lesion in my mouth at the age of 19. I had to get it surgically removed and thankfully it was benign. However, the life lesson it taught me was that trying to escape reality through chewing tobacco was not a healthy life choice. I chewed tobacco from probably 17 all the way up until I was 19. I quit right after I got cancer.
After cancer surgery, I tossed out the dip I still had away, only to go out and purchase cigarettes. Like that was any better; I still had an addiction to feed.

I continued to smoke until I was around 22, then I tried to go back to dipping; however, I ended up giving tobacco up entirely for the rest of my life and not letting my addiction control me.
Somewhere between 22 and 23, I made the decision to leave the apartment my grandma helped me get to go hitchhiking. I left the tiny one-bedroom apartment in the Spring of 2016 to explore the huge, vast world around me on foot. I learned to survive by dumpster diving and eating food people didn't finish eating at fast food places.

The easiest way to get food most days was for me to sit around a restaurant like Sonic, and watch for people who seemed decent/clean to toss their trash in the garage can. Normally, it was an elderly couple or someone older as there was guaranteed to be some untouched, warm tater tots/fries. I still had my standards, ironic to say, but I didn't always eat the food left in the trash. It was better than going hungry though.

In a span of weeks, I had hitchhiked from the top of Kentucky down to the border of Tennessee. For the most part, hitchhiking was everything I hoped for: free, full of adventure, and challenging. With all adventure came danger at some point though. Don't get me wrong, there was more nice people out there than bad as I was given meals, money, or rides more often than encountering someone rude. There was one event that occurred that scared me enough to convince me into going back to live with my grandparents one final time.

It started off at a gas station where one male offered me a ride to a nearby major city, which I gladly accepted as I was trying to get as far as I could. I wanted to see everything there was to see. Once we got far enough from the gas station that would have took at least 1 hour of me walking to get there, the man turned onto this back gravel road with a large brick house nearby. A lady came out of the house at that time, telling the man he couldn't be driving back there. The gravel road actually went into the woods, which I'm assuming the lady owned. Needless to say, the guy told me to hop out after that.

What made it scary was the man telling me his friends would be around soon to pick me up. I'm guessing the guy was worried the lady seen me with him and that's why he told me to get out. Anyways, I was stuck now on this back lonely road so I just started walked towards where the city was supposed to be. About fifteen minutes later, this silver car drove up from behind me with two men inside. The men weren't exactly dressed for warm weather as it looked like they were trying to keep their faces unseen with toboggans on at 3 in the afternoon in late spring.

As these two men were talking to me, telling me to get in their car, I noticed one of them messing with the child safety lock on the back door. I've always been the observant type of person, taking in my surroundings and environment for any threats or danger. I knew something was up now. That child safety prevented the door from being opened by someone inside.
The alarms went off in my head, causing me to know not to get into that vehicle with them. Shit, I was ready to drop my damn backpack and take off running into the fields. I was polite with the men who looked like convicts to me, thanking them for stopping to pick me up but not accepting the ride. I was scared the men were going to try something;

but they drove off and I continued walking on the road. I went to a nearby house, begging the couple that lived there to give me a ride to the nearest city. I was really scared the men would come back for me.

The couple was nice enough to give a ride to the city; from there, I called my grandma a few days later and asked them to come pick me up. My grandma hadn't heard from me in weeks now, so she drove all the way to Bowling Green, to pick me up. I went back and lived with my grandma for the rest of the spring into the late summer. At that point, I went and moved in with great-grandmother sometime during June of 2016. My great-grandma taught me how to drive a vehicle, she helped me get my education, and I could never thank her enough for what she did for me. She gave me a place to stay and lit a fire under my ass to get my life together.

After getting my education, the first thing I did was go out and get a job. I had finally, with the help of my great-grandma, got my own car for my birthday; and my brother, who I didn't see eye-to-eye with, ended up getting caught making meth labs. So, he got sent off to the county jail. To this day, he's a convicted inmate in the State Penitentiary. Whatever happened to my other brother you ask? By the time he finally turned 18, he got sick and my stepdad's shit so he went and moved in with his girl somewhere in Kentucky.

In case you're wondering what happened to my
parents, my mother is not doing so well these days.
All those years of smoking and eating horribly have
taken a toll on her body and now she's stuck on a
breathing machine. I have told her that I forgave
her for all the stuff she did.

There's been more than one occasion where she's
been on the phone crying to my grandmother,
saying that she wish she could change everything
and take it all back. She wonders to this day why I
don't visit, and it's because if I did visit she would
start getting her temper with me and I'm just too old
for that. I am too old to deal with her again. So,
again, I'm sorry, mom; I love you, but we mix like
fire and gasoline.
My grandmother always asks me why I never go
and visit my mother. She tells me that I should
honor my mother, but I don't blame my
grandmother because she wasn't there. She didn't
know what I was going through. It's not her fault for
thinking I should just forgive and forget. I have
forgave my mom; it's just not easy to forget years of
abuse though. My grandma's only trying to do the
right thing like she always does.

I'm a grown man now. I don't try to dwell much on
the past life I no longer live. I have my own house;
my own success; I went and I finally found
somebody who I care about very dearly, my wife.
And I'm happy now. I've learned that if you ever
want to get to happiness, if you ever want to have

a great life; you'll have to go through the pain to get it. Pain has taught me great lessons in life, one of those being that we all strive to avoid pain and seek pleasure. It's pain that changes a human being.

Know that if you are out there and you are a victim of the same violence and abuse that I was as a child, there is help out there.

Go to: https://www.thehotline.org/ or call them at 1800-799-7233

You're not alone in the abuse. There is help.

Printed in Great Britain
by Amazon